# HOW TO MAKE COLLABORATION WORK

*Powerful Ways to Build Consensus,
Solve Problems,
and Make Decisions*

# DAVID STRAUS

BERRETT-KOEHLER PUBLISHERS, INC.
San Francisco

Berrett-Koehler Publishers, Inc.
235 Montgomery, Suite 650
San Francisco, CA 94104-2916
Tel: 415-288-0260      Fax: 415-362-2512
Website: www.bkconnection.com

**ORDERING INFORMATION**

*Individual sales.* Berrett-Koehler publications are available through most bookstores. They can also be ordered direct from Berrett-Koehler Publishers by calling, toll-free: 800-929-2929; fax 802-864-7626.

*Quantity sales.* Special discounts are available on quantity purchases by corporations, associations, and others. For details, contact the "Special Sales Department" at the Berrett-Koehler address above.

*Orders for college textbook/course adoption use.* Please contact Berrett-Koehler Publishers toll-free: 800-929-2929; fax 802-864-7626.

*Orders by U.S. trade bookstores and wholesalers.* Please contact Publishers Group West, 1700 Fourth Street, Berkeley, CA 94710; 510-528-1444; 1-800-788-3123; fax 510-528-9555.

Printed in the United States of America

Berrett-Koehler books are printed on long-lasting acid-free paper. When it is available, we choose paper that has been manufactured by environmentally responsible processes. These may include using trees grown in sustainable forests, incorporating recycled paper, minimizing chlorine in bleaching, or recycling the energy produced at the paper mill.

**Library of Congress Cataloging-in-Publication Data**
Straus, David.
    How to make collaboration work : powerful ways to build consensus, solve problems, and make decisions / by David Straus
        p.   cm.
    Includes bibliographical references and index.
    ISBN 1-57675-128-7
    1. Teams in the workplace.   2. Group decision making.   3. Group problem solving.
4. Cooperativeness.   I. Title.
    HD66.S772 2002
    658.4'036—dc21
2002018470

07   06   05   04   03   02      10   9   8   7   6   5   4   3   2   1

Text designer: Detta Penna
Copyeditor: Marguerite Rigoglioso
Indexer: Joan Dickey

*To my father,*
*Donald B. Straus*
*A pioneer in the field*

# Contents

# Foreword

I first met David Straus more than thirty years ago. I was involved with the Coro Foundation, an organization that focused on experience-based, graduate education in public affairs. We were committed to training leaders to function effectively in an ever more complex world. Coro was located on the wide-open top floor of a South of Market Street warehouse in San Francisco, in the center of what would become the dot.com world many years later. We didn't know it then, but across the floor from us, a small group of visionaries would have a profound effect not only on what we did and how we did it, but on much of the world as well. David was their organizer and leader. They called themselves Interaction Associates.

It seems difficult to believe it now, but in 1971, terms such as "facilitator" and "process management" were not part of the common language, let alone "win-win" or "explicit group memory." Nobody was taping sheets of paper on the wall and "recording." Collaboration was probably more associated with giving secrets to enemies than with sharing power with colleagues. Leadership and control were not dissimilar concepts. David was searching for new ways of "problem solving," for processes and methodologies that involved multiple parties working together at the same time and in the same place, and that truly respected and honored the widely diverse ideas and input of as many of those involved—i.e., the stakeholders—as possible. The notion that the process would be run most effectively by a highly trained neutral was revolutionary, and yet it made sense. We were mesmerized by all that was happening on the other side of our warehouse floor, and we were invited to watch and participate.

From my vantage point in 1971, I had the privilege of observing David and his colleagues as they developed, pushed, reinvented, refined, and experimented with the field of collaborative problem solving. David was constantly finding new venues and applications for his ever-expanding skills, techniques, and theories. No challenge was too big or too small for the ever-evolving Interaction Method, whether it be the nonadversarial divorce of a friend or the redesign of an entire community.

I became fast friends with David and his wife-to-be, Patricia, and, later, his entire family. Subsequently, as Interaction Associates grew, I joined the board of directors of the company and had the chance to participate in a very small way in the growth of both the for-profit and the nonprofit sides of the company. By that time, I had become the CEO of a grantmaking foundation and found that some of the best ideas and projects presented to me were closely related to and informed by the work of Interaction Associates (IA). Soon other foundations were supporting the field as well. One of the most important examples was the development of the field of "alternative dispute resolution," which has come to include everything from neighborhood justice centers and school-based programs to highly sophisticated, multi-lateral efforts undertaken by organizations such as the Carter Center (which was staffed with the help of Bill Spencer, a former Interaction Associates partner). Over my years of friendship and work with David, when the business side of Interaction Associates was stressed, I was fond of asking, "Just what kind of organization is Interaction Associates? A business? A religion? A think-tank?" The answer, of course, is that it's all of the above and more. Interaction Associates has been an ongoing experiment in modeling how to facilitate leadership, how to grow the field of consensus-driven decision making, and how to listen to and respect every voice.

For David, it's been the work of a lifetime—from Harvard to Berkeley and back again, going around the world in the process. His training in architecture and design has played out on the largest imaginable stage. A new language has been created. New values are now widely held. The tens of thousands who have participated in Interaction Associates' training program, and the hundreds of thousands who have read *How to Make Meetings Work*, are only the tip of the iceberg. David Straus's life work is a gift to us all.

Thomas C. Layton
President
Wallace A. Gerbode Foundation
San Francisco

# Preface

In 1992, a colleague and I traveled to Austria to conduct a five-day training course in meeting facilitation for fifteen university professors from Eastern Europe. These men and women had lived their whole lives under totalitarian regimes, which had only recently been overthrown. They were hungry for knowledge about nonadversarial approaches to solving problems and resolving conflicts. The course went well, and the participants were enthusiastic about the concepts they had learned.

A year later, these same individuals came to the United States to learn from us how to train others to be facilitators. I was thrilled to be hosting in our beautiful city of San Francisco these intelligent and enthusiastic people, who had been so gracious to us during our time in Austria.

My colleagues and I had gone to considerable effort and expense to prepare for this train-the-trainer program. We developed a detailed manual for each participant, similar to what we put together for our corporate clients. These thick three-ring binders outlined exactly how to run a facilitation training program—what to say when, what exercises to conduct during each segment of the program, and so forth.

Midway through the workshop—and much to our surprise—our Eastern European friends politely handed us back the training manuals. "We know that your course is built on a few powerful ideas," they explained. *"Make sure that we have those ideas in our hearts, and then we will sing."*

The words of these dedicated men and women came back to me as I struggled to find a way to organize the material for this book. It was a real challenge to figure out how to capture on paper what I had learned about collaboration over the last thirty years, in a way that would be useful to anyone interested in helping his or her group, organization, or community to work more collaboratively. I had enough material for at least ten "how-to" books on the tools and techniques of collaboration at different levels of society, from the interpersonal to the whole systems level. I had already co-written one such book, on small-group problem solving (*How to Make Meetings Work*, with Michael Doyle). I wanted this book to appeal to a broad audience—not just organizational consultants, but leaders, managers, supervisors, and rank-and-file members of every manner of organization and community. I also wanted to share something of my own personal journey and that of the company I founded, Interaction Associates. I needed a way to boil down to its essence what I knew to be true about collaboration. Then I remembered the words of the Eastern Europeans: *"a few powerful ideas . . . . "*

## A Few Powerful Ideas

So I've organized this book around a few powerful ideas, or principles, that, if grasped in your heart and mind, will allow you to harness the power of collaborative action for yourself and your group, organization, or community. If you understand these principles and the values underlying them, you will have the freedom to implement them in your own way in a variety of situations. In short, you will be able to make your own music.

At first glance, the ideas in this book may seem too simple, too obvious. Indeed, they represent the *distillation* of more than thirty years of learning and practice applying the concepts of collaboration in almost every imaginable context. So they are very "concentrated." My lifelong goal has been to demystify these concepts—to express them as simply as possible, and to give them away. But there is a risk. They can appear too simple, and therefore too easy to dismiss. I hope you will see, when you begin to explore their implications, that these simple ideas are in fact profound.

Although the principles themselves are the stars of this book, I also take the time to explain the impact they have had on me, my organization, and our clients. I offer my own life as one context for observing what happens when you try to grasp, as well as fail to heed, these principles. I offer my company, Interaction Associates, as an illustration of one consulting firm's struggle to practice the collaborative values and principles it preaches. And I offer the experience of my colleagues and our clients as examples of how these principles can be applied to a wide variety of situations in the private, public, and nonprofit sectors. These stories illustrate the obvious importance and promise of the principles.

Those of you who are organizational consultants or facilitators, or who have led collaborative planning processes of one form or another, are probably familiar with many of the principles in this book. The principles evolved from the work of many people inside and outside of Interaction Associates. I don't claim ownership of them. However, I invite you to take a journey with me back to the roots of these principles. For example, we will reconnect with the origins of the concept of *group memory* and think about how an idea like this might be implemented in the new world of virtual collaboration. The exercise of writing this book has given me an opportunity to reflect on the essence of these principles, and, in the process, I have gained some new insights.

Those of you who are new to the concepts in this book and are interested in improving the quality of collaboration in some aspect of your life will find the book to be more substantial than a simple introduction, yet easy to understand and put into practice. (Indeed, the final third of the book focuses specifically on how to put the principles to use.) You may notice, too, that I don't spend much time trying to convince you of the need for collaboration. I'm assuming that you know collaboration is necessary and that you are already engaged in collaborative work in your organization or community. Instead, I focus on the major challenges you are likely facing in those endeavors and offer a few powerful principles which, if you grasp them in your heart and mind, will help you to collaborate with success.

Before you get into the substance of the book, I want to point out that collaboration is not value-free. It's based on some mental models and core values about people and what is possible when people work together. The ideas in the book require certain *heart-sets*, as well as *mind-sets*, to be properly implemented. Collaboration assumes, for example, the dignity and value of every human being, and each person's right to be involved in decisions that affect his or her life. I try to surface these underlying values periodically, so that you can understand the obligations you assume if you choose to initiate a collaborative process. If you act consistently with these values, you will avoid the potential abuses of the power of collaborative action.

My intention in this book is to present a constellation of ideas about collaboration. Each idea is powerful in and of itself and speaks to both our hearts and minds. Taken together, these actionable ideas offer a hopeful view of the world and of people's role in it. They present a vision of a better world in which people with differing interests can work together constructively to make decisions and solve problems, and even tackle the complex, systemic issues our society faces. They point us toward a more humane and healthy work environment—toward what is possible.

*David Straus*
*Cambridge, Massachusetts*
*June 2002*

# Acknowledgements

This book tells a collective story as well as a personal one. Many people inside and outside of Interaction Associates and the Interaction Institute for Social Change participated in developing and implementing these powerful ideas about collaboration. I want to acknowledge those who took time out of their busy schedules to offer valuable input and feedback on my drafts: Terry Amsler, Geoff Ball, Paul Botticello, Courtney Bourns, Nancy Brodsky, David D. Chrislip, Janice Cohen, Jay Cone, David M. Ehrmann, Caroline J. Fisher, Mary Gelinas, Gessner Geyer, Peter Gibb, Jamie Harris, Charles Heckscher, Marianne Hughes, Gerald Leader, Robert Mnookin, Ann O'Brien, Beth O'Neill, Cynthia Parker, John Parr, Heather Payne, Alex Plinio, Michael Reidy, Thomas Rice, Barry Rosen, Robert Ryan, Ray Shonholtz, Cary Sneider, William Spencer, Donald B. Straus, Lawrence Susskind, and Allan Wallis. Thank you to Lisa Kimball, who hosted a Web conference to support virtual collaboration and dialogue about early drafts of this book. I also want to thank Berrett-Koehler's external reviewers for their honest and helpful comments: Marcia Dazko, Chester Delaney, Kathleen Epperson, Tom Heuerman, and Andrea Markowitz. Special thanks goes to Jay Cone, who encouraged me to write this book and reintroduced me to Steve Piersanti. Thank you, Steve, for being so supportive, encouraging, and direct. To my wife, Patty, thank you for being so patient and understanding as I retreated into my office to write. And finally, while I take responsibility for the quality of the content of this book, the quality of the writing I attribute to my skillful collaborator and editor, Jennifer Thomas-Larmer. Thank you all.

# The Power of Collaborative Action

People in nearly every occupation and every walk of life have to work and make decisions *collaboratively*. Collaboration is required at every level of every organization—be it a corporation, small business, nonprofit organization, educational institution, government agency, or legislative body. And collaboration takes place not only within these organizations, but also between and among them. Collaborative action is required, for example, when:

- a senior management team needs to figure out how to cut expenses by 15 percent;

- an organization wants to define its purpose and vision, or develop a strategic plan;

- a team in an advertising agency needs to design a new ad campaign;

- administrative staffers have to make logistical arrangements for an important company retreat;

- a group of teachers must jointly develop a new curriculum;

- nonprofit advocacy groups want to form a coalition to lobby for a particular issue;

- a number of social service agencies must determine how to coordinate their services;

- a government agency needs to update its policy for regulating a toxic pollutant; or

- a couple decides they want to build a new house.

The list could go on and on. These and so many other activities require collaboration. They require people to work together to plan, solve problems, and/or make decisions before action can be taken.

You undoubtedly collaborate all the time—primarily at work, but also at home, in your volunteer activities, at your child's school. You may not think of what you are doing as collaboration, but if you have to get the support and agreement of others before you can take action of some kind, then you are collaborating.

Even in those cases in which you supposedly have the power to act unilaterally—in which you can simply make a decision and then act on it—you probably know that you still have to work collaboratively. Perhaps you need to collaborate because, for example, too many people have the power to block the implementation of your decision or solution. Perhaps power has become spread out (or *lateralized*). Or, the potential costs of acting unilaterally may be too high. You could force a decision, but you would meet with so much resistance and create so much ill will that you would erode your base of support. Perhaps your colleagues, employees, or constituents simply expect or demand that you act more inclusively and collaboratively. Or, maybe you don't have the skills or knowledge to make the decision or solve the problem by yourself. You may need to include and cooperate with others in order to make the best decision possible.

Whatever the situation, it's quite clear that we all have to work collaboratively with others.

But let's face it, our experience in trying to reach agreement with others is often unpleasant. We don't enjoy it at all. It's hard. Our efforts often seem ineffective. Collaboration typically involves meetings, and no one likes meetings. We make jokes about how "a camel is a horse designed by a committee." We are cynical when we hear that a politician has appointed a fifty-person "blue-ribbon panel" to develop consensus recommendations, because we assume either that it's a stalling tactic or that the panel is stacked with people who share the politician's point of view. After all, how could fifty people with diverging opinions possibly reach consensus?

The problems that can arise in a meeting in which collaboration is supposed to take place are numerous and familiar. People may talk over each other or interrupt each other. Certain individuals—by virtue of their positions or their personalities—may dominate or manipulate the conversation. Participants may be unable to stay focused on one topic at a time. The conversation may veer all over the place, causing people to become exasperated. Perhaps there's no clear picture of what the group's goal is, or how the group is going to get there. Or participants may realize, midway through a discussion, that some key people are missing—that whatever they decide could be "shot down" by someone outside the process. These examples of meeting problems are magnified when a collaborative effort involves large numbers of people and multiple meetings over time.

The fact is, however, there's nothing inherently unpleasant about collaboration. Working together to solve a problem, envision a future, or make a decision can actually be an enjoyable and even *energizing* experience.

I don't make that statement lightly. I base it on thirty years of trial-and-error experience in the field of collaborative problem solving.

My colleagues and clients and I have proven, time and time again, that collaborative action can be a powerful experience. A well-managed collaborative effort is like a chemical reaction that creates far more energy than it consumes. It makes you feel energized, not drained. We call this phenomenon the *Interaction Effect*. When a group is in alignment about its direction (where it is trying to go), its commitment (the will it possesses to get there), and its capability (the skills and knowledge it has to complete its journey), there is a release of energy. Not only are team members energized by the process, but so is the surrounding organization or community. It's this energy that fuels an extended collaborative effort and keeps it going during rough times.

Even more important, *collaboration works.* If you understand how problem solving works and adhere to a few basic principles, it is possible to make decisions and develop solutions that everyone can support. Through collaborative action, you can produce higher-quality ideas and solutions than you can if you work by yourself. People who are affected by a potential decision, have relevant information and skills, or have the power to block a decision are more likely to support that decision if they have had a hand in making it.

Furthermore, I believe that stakeholder voice is a basic right of individuals in healthy workplaces and democratic societies. Collaborative action is a natural outgrowth of this right and a demonstration of respect for human dignity.

So, why is it that this potentially energizing experience is so unpleasant for so many people?

In short, because most people don't know how to collaborate effectively. Collaboration needs to be learned. It's an art, really, that is based on a few powerful principles. But most people aren't familiar with those principles. They've never been taught them.

Think back to your early education. If it was anything like mine, you were taught in school to value and strive for individual success. You studied, took tests, gave presentations, and were graded and given awards individually. Group work was neither measured nor rewarded. Team sports may have provided some antidote to all of this "I" focus, but, even there, weren't you mostly encouraged to develop individual prowess for the sake of the team? That's not the same as solving problems or making decisions collaboratively, which is what's demanded of us in today's workplaces and communities.

Another reason we don't know how to collaborate is that our schools focused (and still do focus) on teaching us *content*, not *process*. In school, we were taught *what* to learn—what facts and formulas to memorize—but we were rarely taught *how* to learn. Likewise, we were given problems to work out, and we were eventually given the answers to those problems, but we were seldom taught explicitly how to solve the problems—what mental or physical processes to use. And since we didn't learn how to solve problems individually, it's no wonder we have trouble solving problems collaboratively.

In this book, therefore, I hope to help fill this gap in our educational background. I hope to help you learn about *the process of collaborative problem solving*. And I hope to demystify the process and show you that it really isn't hard or unpleasant. It really can be enjoyable and energizing!

## What Collaboration IS

When I use the synonymous terms *collaboration, collaborative action*, and *collaborative problem solving*, I am referring to the process people employ when working together in a group, organization, or community to plan, create, solve problems, and make decisions.

Clearly, I'm not using the word *collaboration* in its negative sense, as in collaborating or working with the enemy. I have done enough work in Europe and former Communist countries to know that *collaboration* often viscerally evokes an image of collusion. In those situations, I have found that the word *cooperation* has more of the intended meaning of working toward a positive outcome together. Also, using the term *collaborative action* sometimes helps to avoid this pitfall.

Then there are the words *problem* and *problem solving*. As I will discuss in Chapter 2, I use these words in their most general and inclusive sense. I define a *problem* as "a situation someone wants to change." *Problem solving*, then, is simply situation changing. It encompasses decision making and planning and all kinds of creative activities such as designing, exploring new opportunities, engaging in appreciative inquiry, visioning, learning, and communicating.

Problem solving, and specifically collaborative problem solving, is a *process* that is largely independent of *content*. The distinction between process and content is very important for the message of this book. I once asked a class of sixth graders for definitions of these two words. One boy raised his hand and said, "It's just like chewing gum. Chewing is my process. Gum is my content. I can chew all sorts of things. Gum is what I happen to be chewing now." He was exactly right. Process is the *how* (chewing), content is the *what* (gum).

This book is about the *process* of collaborative problem solving. The process is content-independent. It can be applied to any kind of issue, subject matter, or opportunity. If you become aware of this process and grasp the principles in this book, you will be able to harness the power of collaborative action in almost any situation.

## How This Book Is Organized

I hope to inspire and empower you to collaborate successfully with others in your personal and professional lives. Toward this end, I have organized the book into three parts.

Part I deals with the important meta-idea of *human problem solving*. While the focus of this book is more on collaboration than on problem solving, per se, it's important to understand some basic facts about the trial-and-error nature of human problem solving in order to understand how humans can solve problems *together*. If you are confronted by an immediate collaboration-related problem, you may want to jump to the most relevant chapter in Part II. However, I urge you to return to Part I in order to build a base of understanding for the ideas that follow.

Guided by my experience with the Eastern European trainers who wanted "a few powerful ideas," in Part II I have tried to distill what I know into *five principles of collaborative problem solving*. Each principle speaks to both our hearts and minds. Each principle can also be applied to any scale of collaborative problem solving, from interpersonal and small-group processes to organization- and community-wide processes. Taken together, the five principles offer an actionable paradigm, a way of looking at the world that is hopeful. What has been so exciting for me to witness is that these principles simply work. They have been applied successfully in hundreds of organizations and communities both in the United States and around the world.

Each principle addresses the specific questions and challenges you are likely to confront when trying to design and manage a process of collaboration. These include:

- With whom do I need to collaborate? Do I really have to involve people who oppose my ideas?

- What if there are many people involved—many organizations, departments, or organizations? How would we ever get them together? How would the process work?

- If we actually get everyone in the same room together, who will run the meeting and how?

- How do we keep the group from spinning its wheels or getting bogged down?

- What if we are spread out geographically all over the country or world?

- How do we make decisions? What happens if we can't easily come to agreement? Do we vote?

The following is a preview of the five principles:

- **Involve the Relevant Stakeholders**. One of the biggest mistakes people make in trying to work collaboratively is to exclude a key individual or interest group. "We weren't consulted," is an oft-heard complaint that prevents collaborative work from succeeding. So, you need to determine who the stakeholders are and how to involve them. In general, the power of collaborative action comes from inclusion, not exclusion. It's far more powerful to have someone inside the tent than outside. The long-term payoff is immeasurable.

- **Build Consensus Phase by Phase.** Consensus has been reached when everyone agrees to support a decision. And agreement doesn't just happen; it has to be built, phase by phase. Working face-to-face to build agreements is significantly different from negotiating through a mediator. And consensus building always needs a fallback decision-making process—some way of coming to a decision if consensus can't be reached.

- **Design a Process Map.** People become anxious in the face of too much uncertainty. Before agreeing to collaborate, they will probably want some sense of what they're getting into. What is needed is a clear means of designing and managing an open-ended process of collaboration. The most powerful way to do this is to create a *process map*—a visual representation of a collaborative process. The process map serves the same function for a long-term collaborative process that an agenda does for a single meeting. It defines the order of activities and gives participants a sense of how these activities fit into the larger context.

- **Designate a Process Facilitator.** Not surprisingly, much of the business of collaboration takes place when people come together to talk. And, time and time again, we see and hear about leaders trying to run their own meetings. This is often a mistake! As a leader, it's difficult for you to be neutral about how a meeting is run when you care deeply about and are accountable for the decisions made in that meeting. It's essential that you separate process leadership from content leadership and create a new role, that of facilitator. A facilitator is a neutral process guide and servant to the group.

- **Harness the Power of Group Memory**. Data overload, repetition, wheel-spinning, and lack of focus are all symptoms of bad meetings. And they all have the same solution: chart pads and colored markers. If you rearrange the seats in a semicircle, tape sheets of newsprint on the wall, and have someone serve as a recorder, these common meeting problems will be prevented. The record, or *group memory*, that is created in front of the group is one of the most simple—and powerful—tools of collaboration.

Part III of the book looks to the future, exploring what happens if you apply these principles of collaboration *throughout a whole organization or community*. How would your role as a leader have to change? How can you create a culture of collaboration in an entire corporation or community, and what is the effect if you do? I cover some of the evidence that suggests that collaborative organizations and collaborative communities function better and are healthier places in which to work and live than their more traditional, command-and-control counterparts. I also offer some thoughts on how and where you might begin to put these powerful ideas about collaboration into action right away. The following is a preview of the chapters in Part III:

- **Facilitative Leadership**. Collaborative action must be enabled, promoted, and supported by leaders. And the kind of leadership required is fundamentally different from the old command-and-control model. Facilitative leadership involves new practices. If you want to build a collaborative culture in your organization or community, you must be able to model the mind-sets and values of collaborative action.

- **Collaborative Organizations**. Collaborative action is not
  only an effective approach for resolving specific, discrete issues—it can become the norm for an entire organization.
  But you have to know how to scale it up, how to institution-
  alize a culture of collaboration. You also need a clear image
  of how a collaborative organization operates. A number of
  organizations have made significant progress in this direction. There is preliminary evidence that these collaborative
  organizations are more adaptive and responsive to changes
  in their external environments than their more traditional
  counterparts. They also appear to be more productive and
  healthier workplaces. To reinforce and support collaboration, several organizational components have to be brought
  into alignment, including leadership, structure, strategy,
  support technologies, the reward system, core skills, and corporate culture.

- **Collaborative Communities**. Traditional democratic
  processes are inadequate for resolving the complex, systemic
  issues that our communities face today. Too many interests
  are affected, and the issues are often too ill-defined to be decided by a yes/no vote on a referendum. Multiparty collaborative action holds the promise of a more inclusive and
  productive process for tackling important public issues than
  simple majority voting. It is also possible to build a culture
  of collaboration at the community or city level. Several communities have made impressive progress in this direction.
  (Portland, Maine, provides a great example.) But just as with
  creating any type of cultural change, several kinds of interventions are required.

- **Where to Go from Here**. The place to begin working collaboratively is in your heart. Try to hold in your heart two
  powerful ideas: (1) every human being has the right to be involved in decisions that affect his or her life, and (2) with
  good process, people can generate more creative and com-

10

prehensive solutions collaboratively than they can by themselves. Mastery of the tools and techniques essential for successful collaboration will follow. With learning and practice, you can make collaboration work for you. It's effective, it's energizing, and it is the right thing to do.

## The Context

Throughout the book, I'll be drawing on examples from my personal and professional life, as well as from the work of my colleagues. So, I need to offer a little context. I will frequently refer to the company I founded in 1969, Interaction Associates (IA). IA has been a wonderful vehicle for developing and testing the principles of collaborative action. A mission-driven organization from its inception, IA has endeavored *to empower people in organizations and communities to achieve their most noble aspirations by demonstrating the power and transferring the skills of collaborative action.* We have assisted a wide variety of clients in both the private and public sectors in the United States and around the world in applying the principles and tools of collaborative problem solving. As IA has grown to more than seventy-five full-time employees distributed geographically in several offices, the company itself has become one of the most interesting and challenging contexts within which to implement the ideas and values of collaboration.

For example, from the beginning I was faced with issues of equity and shared responsibility within the organization. As the founder and first shareholder of the company, I had the option of holding on to ownership and control and only giving up stock when challenged by key employees. This is the traditional approach to building wealth and retaining control in privately-owned service firms. However, consistent with the spirit of the 1960s, I was committed to finding a different path, to making Interaction Associates into a collaborative partnership. I quickly learned that there was no such thing as "almost equal." As long as I held one more share than someone else, we were not equals. As long as I retained 51 percent of the shares, collaborative decision making depended on my consent.

So, by the second year I made the great and irreversible leap to a governance and ownership structure of a partnership-like corporation, in which full partners owned exactly the same amount of stock. Such stock was purchased and sold internally at "book value" (i.e., the lowest possible cost without giving the stock away). Thus was launched a social experiment in shared responsibility and collaboration. I am somewhat controlling by nature, so this organizational structure has forced me to trust the process of collaborative action and build faith in my own powers of influence and facilitative leadership.

The challenge of having to apply the principles of collaboration to the way we live and work together at IA has been a source of great learning and satisfaction. We are at our best when our actions are congruent with our professed principles and values. Our clients notice and appreciate this. Our unique governance structure has even withstood the comings and goings of a number of partners over the years.

Just recently, Interaction Associates transitioned from a partnership model to a broader employee-ownership arrangement, in which the shareholders elect a board. That board, in turn, hires someone from within the company to be CEO, who then leads and manages all of us.

Another organization from which I will draw examples for this book is the Interaction Institute for Social Change (IISC). Early on, we at IA saw that there was a huge, unmet demand in the nonprofit and community sectors for the collaborative skills and tools we were offering. These organizations simply could not afford to pay corporate rates for consulting and training services. Over the years we had created, with mixed success, a number of nonprofit "sister" organizations to try to meet this need. But it wasn't until 1993, thanks to the efforts of my friend Thomas Rice, our president at the time, that we hit on a powerful and effective model to deepen and formalize our commitment to social justice. We created the nonprofit IISC and committed ten percent of our pretax profits and up to ten paid days of every IA employee's time to the IISC. The work and organizational culture of the IISC, which now has a full-time staff of eighteen people, have offered vivid contexts for witnessing the many ways in which collaborative action can produce powerful, positive effects on peoples' lives.

## A Process View of the World

Before we dive into the topic of human problem solving, I want to share one mental model that has been very powerful in my life and helps to explain how I got from "there" to "here." My formal graduate education was in architecture. Frustration over how architecture was taught drove me to explore what was known about the processes of human problem solving. During my studies at the Harvard Graduate School of Design, I began to see the world through "process eyes," which was for me a kind of paradigm shift. Connections began to occur to me that did not seem obvious before. What I was learning about individual and group problem solving seemed to be relevant to what should be taught in schools; how groups, organizations, and communities could solve problems; and how technology could be used to augment group problem solving. I began to see that even the intersections between the areas of training, consulting, and augmentation technology defined interesting and relevant fields, as Figure 1 on the next page illustrates.

The initial idea behind the founding of Interaction Associates was to see if some synergy and competitive advantage could be gained by becoming involved in all these different areas at the same time. Creating the company also satisfied my own desire to have an influence on many different kinds of societal problems. By defining my role as a *tool giver* in the fields of training, consulting, and augmentation, I could help people in organizations and

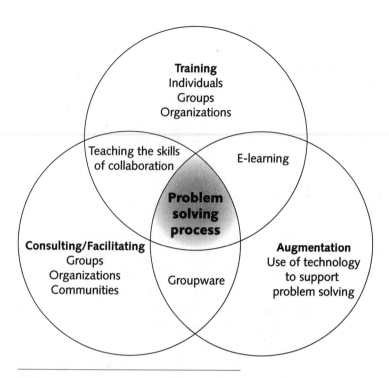

**Figure 1:** A process view of the world

communities become *architects of their own futures,* to solve their own problems.

My hope is that as you read this book, you, too, will have some of the same insights I had and will begin to see the world through "process eyes."

# Part I

# The Fundamentals

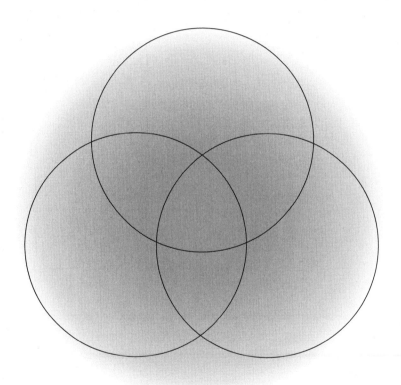

# Chapter 1

# The Process of Human Problem Solving

In 1965, I entered the architecture program at Harvard Graduate School of Design (HGSD). The basic method of teaching design at HGSD, it turned out, was to assign students to design a certain type of building or space and then critique the designs. The critiques were very formal and were modeled after the process an architect might go through in trying to sell an idea to a potential client. The students presented their designs to a panel of faculty members and professional architects. During these critiques, and during class, there was little discussion of the creative *process*—of how we came up with the designs. In fact, there was no accepted language to discuss design methodologies at all. Instead, the professors were mainly interested in the *content* of our designs.

About halfway through my first year, I began to think something was wrong with my eyes. The drawings on my drafting board looked blurred. I had trouble reading. Panicked, I made an appointment with a recommended optometrist.

After examining my eyes, the doctor led me into his office, motioned for me to sit in a comfortable chair, and then posed one of the most insightful questions I've ever been asked. "Your eyes are fine," he said. "What is it that you don't want to see?"

I suddenly realized what it was that I didn't want to see, that I was unconsciously denying. Even though I was paying for a graduate education in architecture, no one was going to teach me explicitly how to design. No one was going to identify and make visible the mental processes of design.

This flash of insight marked, for me, the beginning of my own *process awareness.* This moment was the first step in my lifelong journey to uncover and demystify the processes of individual and group problem-solving, and to transfer these concepts and tools to others.

In this chapter, I hope to shed some light on how individuals solve problems. This information is fundamental to an understanding of collaboration—of how individuals solve problems *together.* It's simply not possible to practice collaborative problem solving effectively if you have no understanding of human problem solving in general. This chapter is a bit heavier on theory than the other chapters in the book, because it serves as a basis for all that follows. To make it as accessible as possible, I use the story of my own experience discovering these concepts and learning their relevance to collaborative action.

## Some Definitions

In the Introduction, I defined *collaborative problem solving* as "the process people employ when working together in a group, organization, or community to plan, create, solve problems, and make decisions." I also talked about what I meant by *collaboration.* Here, I want to say more about the *problem solving* part of the term.

For some people, a *problem* implies something bad, a situation to avoid. In certain contexts, to focus on problems is seen as attending to the negative, the pathological. So some people substitute the word *opportunity* to emphasize the positive, to look at things on the bright side or to look at the possibilities of the future. But *opportunity solving* and *opportunity finding* are clumsy substitutes for *problem solving*, and there is already a whole literature on *creative problem solving*, so I'm going to continue to use the word *problem* in this book.

In any case, I don't view problems as negative. I define a problem as "a situation that someone wants to change." *Problem solving*, therefore, in its most general sense, is *situation changing* or taking action. It includes most of what we do all day long: communicating, learning, planning, working, and making decisions. At work, for example, you may need to make hiring and firing decisions, communicate with employees, fix quality-control problems, sell your products, and so forth. I would call all of these activities *problems*, since they are all situations you need to change—things you need to do something about.

These situations need not be bad. They include positive situations that you may want to reinforce or increase, like supporting employees to continue their education by offering matching funds to attend training programs. Creating a vision for your organization is also a problem-solving activity just as much as analyzing why the assembly line is causing defects in your products.

Also, under my definition, a problem is only a problem if there is an agent present—someone who cares and wants to take action. If you see your kids arguing and it doesn't bother you, you don't have a problem. Your kids may have a problem, but you don't.

Humans are designed for continual problem solving. If all stimuli are removed from a person's environment (as in an isolated prison cell), often that person will go mad. We are constantly making little changes in our environment, from shifting our sitting position to planning for the future. In this book, then, *problem solving* will refer to all the cognitive processes directed to purposeful action, from perceiving and innovating through planning and decision making.

## My Intellectual Quest

Soon after the revelation that came during my eye exam, I set out to teach myself how to design—how to solve the design problems presented by my professors. I could find no useful books about how to design, and my professors were not very helpful. So I started keeping detailed design notebooks, in which I tried to track my own thought processes, to become more aware and at least "consciously incompetent" about the ways I was attacking a project. I found that when I tried a new design strategy, a different way of looking at a three-dimensional structure, I was suddenly able to do things I couldn't do before. For example, I learned how to draw a *section perspective*, which presents a "slice" through a building and a perspective of what you might see from that point. Through this drawing you see your design in a different way. I also learned how to build simple models out of Styrofoam blocks, with which I could arrange spaces in different ways without having to make new drawings.

In the design notebooks, I documented what I was thinking about when I was stumped, when I kept repeating the same mental process without success. Then, when I discovered another strategy from informal discussions with classmates or professors, I could consciously add it to my growing repertoire of design methodologies. I could also retrace my steps in my design notebooks and see how this new strategy might have helped me break fixation—how it might have served as a way out of a trap in which I had found myself.

I saw clearly that there was a relationship between the strategies I learned and my ability as a problem solver. Each design strategy provided a different way to attack an architectural problem, and the more I learned, the better a designer I became. And yet these strategies were not being explicitly taught.

To satisfy my own curiosity about design methodologies and problem solving, I began to audit courses at Harvard in cognitive psychology with professor Jerome Bruner. In these courses, I was introduced to the work of Allen Newell and Herbert A. Simon from Carnegie-Mellon University, as well as that of Ulrich Neisser.

Neisser (1967) was making a case for cognitive structures, or frameworks, about thinking processes. He maintained that it was possible to describe *how* you were solving a problem, and that it was helpful to do so. Without a framework to describe a subject, he said, it's hard to make distinctions and therefore to acquire and retain new information. For example, if you know nothing about general species of birds (e.g., flycatchers, warblers, wrens, thrushes), they all sort of look the same. When you see a small bird you have never seen before, you might not even know you've never seen it and you probably won't remember much about it. The same is true about problem solving. Without a language of process, without knowing something about the different strategies that can be used to solve problems, it is difficult to learn and acquire new ones.

### There Is No One Right Way!

It was the work of Newell and Simon that provided me with the biggest "aha" of that time, however—one that was to guide my work for years to come. Their writings brought out the simple but powerful fact that human problem solving is an educated trial-and-error process (1972). Put another way, *there is no one right way to solve problems.* We can use a variety of strategies, but none of them will guarantee success. Some of them may be more useful in certain types of situations. But there is no single right way. The implications of this realization are profound. Over the years, my colleagues and I used this understanding as the basis for developing approaches to, and teaching, collaborative problem solving.

## Heuristic vs. Algorithmic Problem Solving

What Newell and Simon (1972) did was to clarify the differences between *heuristic problem solving* and *algorithmic problem solving.*

To illustrate, take the example of trying to find a lost contact lens. The algorithmic approach to searching might involve getting on your hands and knees and systematically crawling back and forth across the floor, trying to cover every square inch. If the contact lens is on the floor as opposed to on the sofa or in your clothes, and if you are very sharp-eyed, you will find your lens this way. However, it may take a very long time. The heuristic approach is to try different strategies in succession. You might start with the common "where were you last" approach. Then you might try to retrace your movements, shake out your clothes, get down on your knees and scan the floor, or turn up the lights to see if you can catch a reflection off the missing lens. Usually one of these heuristic strategies will work quite well and save a great deal of time compared to the algorithmic approach. In short, a *heuristic* is a strategy that is flexible and quick but doesn't guarantee success, while an *algorithm* is an approach that is systematic, rigid, and time consuming, but will ultimately guarantee success.

Newell and Simon discovered a great deal about human problem solving by trying to program computers to solve problems that are reasonably easy for humans. To greatly simplify, Newell and Simon found that there were no simple algorithms to deal with challenges like playing chess or recognizing a face. Such problems require heuristic strategies. What seems to characterize the human brain is our ability to think up heuristics and to be flexible and creative in our application of them.

Take, for example, the anagram of "TABLAERY," in which the challenge is to rearrange the letters so that they spell an English word. The algorithmic approach would be to try every combination of letters and test each to see if it is a word. There are 20,160 possible combinations of the letters, so at a rate of one new combination every ten seconds, it would take you up to fifty-six hours to find a solution this way. Using a heuristic approach, however, many people can come up with an answer in fifteen or twenty minutes. Take a moment and play with the problem, noticing what you do. Notice that you try different ways to solve it, different heuristics. Most people try, for example, rearranging the letters by consonants and vowels, looking for smaller words on which to build, avoiding letter combinations that aren't used in English, and even writing each letter on a separate piece of paper and physically rearranging them. Each of these heuristic strategies may lead you to a solution, but none of them will guarantee success. (See page 33 for the solution—but only after you've tried several heuristics!)

## A Simple Model of Human Problem Solving

So Newell and Simon demonstrated that human problem solving is a trial-and-error process involving choosing a heuristic strategy, testing it, and, if it doesn't work, choosing another. This heuristic cycle is illustrated by the model in Figure 2.

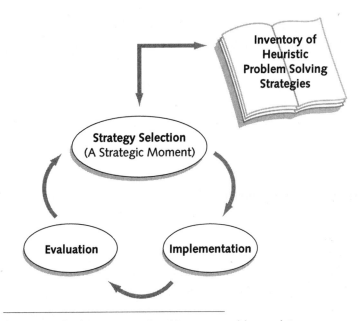

**Figure 2:** The heuristic cycle of human problem solving

The problem-solving cycle begins with what we call a *strategic moment*—that familiar point in time at which whatever you have been trying isn't working anymore. For example, in your search for your contact lens, you may try shaking out your clothes to see if the lens might be caught in the cuffs of your pants. If nothing falls out, you have to try something else. This is the moment at which you consult the repertoire of strategies you have learned, pick one, and implement it. Perhaps, for example, you decide to simply vary the implementation of your current heuristic (e.g., shake out your shirt rather than your pant cuffs), or you may change your approach and select a new strategy. Based on the results, the feedback from your efforts, you evaluate the success or failure of your trial and then you are back to another strategic moment.

This cycle of action/reaction usually happens so quickly that we're not aware of it. It's when we get stuck in a strategic moment that it's helpful to be able to assume conscious control of our problem solving. This is especially true in a group problem-solving situation, as we will see.

So, the great fact I learned in graduate school is that human problem solving is fundamentally a trial-and-error process employing heuristic strategies. There is no one right way. There are no simple algorithms for dealing with most of the open-ended problems we face every day. However, as I was soon to learn, there is a set of very useful heuristics that can be employed.

## A Limited Set of Problem-Solving Heuristics

My own search for heuristics led me to the University of California at Berkeley during my thesis year (1968–69), while I was still registered at the Harvard Graduate School of Design. At this time, the School of Environmental Design at UC Berkeley was a world center for the study of design methodology—of how architects design. Berkeley professor Sim Van der Ryn had received a grant from the National Institute of Mental Health to review the literature on design methodology and try to make some sense of it. He hired me to assist him. It was a perfect opportunity for me to pursue my interest in human problem solving.

I began my research by asking some of Van der Ryn's renowned colleagues to share with me their different design tools. To my surprise, they strongly resisted getting involved in my project. Each of them was sure that he or she had discovered the right approach to design and was not interested in exploring the full range of design methods. So I turned to other sources, reviewing the literature and interviewing researchers from a variety of fields who were exploring the nature of human problem solving.

I began to make a list of the problem-solving methods I uncovered. I discovered that thinkers from very different fields often used essentially the same methods, although they sometimes used different terminology to describe these methods. Indeed, similar methods kept cropping up over and over. I realized that any given problem-solving method could be applied to many different contexts. For example, *brainstorming*, a common way of generating ideas, can be applied to different problems in many different fields. You can brainstorm ideas for creating an ad campaign or solving a calculus problem or finding a place to have dinner.

Like most problem-solving methods, brainstorming involves multiple steps—multiple heuristics. Brainstorming involves, first, *purging* or expressing out loud all the ideas that come into your head; then *listing* or *recording* them on a sheet of paper; and, at the same time, *deferring* evaluation, or not judging them until later. Brainstorming and other problem-solving methods, then, can be understood as "molecules" made up of smaller "atoms." These atoms, or heuristics, can be used by themselves or recombined into many other methods.

Listing, by itself, for example, is a very powerful heuristic. It's the basis of "to do" lists and shopping lists. It's a good way to get ideas out of your head so you can remember them and don't have to keep repeating them to yourself. (As we'll see in Chapter 6, that's why it's so important to record ideas on chart pad paper during meetings—because then people can stop repeating their ideas to each other.)

Each heuristic has many advantages, like any tool. Each also has disadvantages or limitations. While a hammer is great for pounding nails into wood, it's not useful for putting screws in wood, except maybe as a way to get them started. While listing can be useful, it's also sometimes helpful to let an idea germinate—to not express it too quickly.

For my research, I took the list of problem-solving methods and broke these "molecules" into their heuristic "atoms." I gave each heuristic a label or tag—typically an action verb. Wherever possible, I paired each heuristic with its opposite. These heuristic pairs included, for example: "working forward/working backward," "building up/eliminating," and "leaping in/holding back." While my list of problem-solving methods kept getting larger, my list of heuristics grew to sixty-four and then stopped. I decided, using this very simple, unsystematic, and heuristic process, that *there exists a limited set of core heuristics, about sixty-four in total, out of which all of the more complex problem-solving methods can be built.* (A complete list of sixty-four is included in the Resources section at the end of the book.)

## A Pragmatic Theory About Learning Problem-Solving Skills

So in 1969 I came to what was for me a startling and yet reassuring realization: If human problem solving is heuristic and there are a limited number of heuristics, there must be a link between one's repertoire of heuristics and one's ability to solve problems. I began to develop a pragmatic theory about learning and teaching problem-solving skills. It's presented visually in Figure 3.

This theory of learning starts with the premise that (1) your ability as a self-confident, flexible problem solver is dependent on

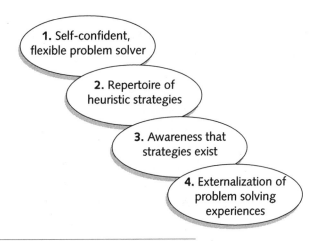

**Figure 3:** A theory about how humans learn problem-solving skills

(2) the repertoire of heuristic strategies that you have learned and are able to apply in a variety of situations. In order to increase your repertoire of heuristic strategies, you must (3) gain awareness that these strategies even exist. And one important way to become aware is by (4) externalizing your problem-solving experiences—that is, thinking out loud—and watching other people externalize theirs. Now, let's look at these elements of the theory in turn, starting with the second one.

### Your Repertoire of Heuristic Strategies

The more heuristics you know, the more effective and creative you will be as a thinker. This is the tool-user analogy: The more tools a carpenter has in his or her toolkit and is able to use skillfully, the more he or she will be able to deal successfully with different types of woodworking problems. The more heuristic thinking tools you have learned and know how to use, the more creative and productive you will be.

## Awareness: The Key to Building Your Repertoire

To increase both the number of heuristics in your tool kit and your ability to use them effectively, you must increase your awareness. Just becoming aware that heuristics exist can help you to demystify individual as well as group problem solving. You can make an inventory of the heuristics you already know and consciously begin to learn new ones. Furthermore, process awareness allows you to become "consciously competent"—to assume control over your choice of problem-solving strategies when necessary.

To help you understand the importance of process awareness, let's consider some sports analogies. Think about playing tennis. Most of the time, when you're playing your best, you're not thinking about your strokes. You are just playing—you're "in the zone"—you're playing with unconscious competence. If your opponent keeps hitting the ball hard to your forehand, however, making you run to reach the shots, and if the only forehand stroke you know is one with topspin, you may have trouble returning these shots with any control. If you have other strokes in your tool kit, however—an underspin slice, for example—then you may be able to handle the pace of the shots and have more control over your returns. But if you don't know the difference between topspin and underspin—if you aren't even aware that there *is* a difference—then you won't be able to make this adjustment in your game. To become a better tennis player, then, you must spend time learning about different kinds of shots—becoming aware of them. Then you must practice them in noncompetitive situations. The more you can groove a stroke so that you don't have to think about it, the more available it will be to you at a crucial moment in a game.

Awareness is critical not only for acquiring new shots, but for keeping yourself in control when things start to go wrong. Watch professional athletes when their game begins to slip. You will see them talking to themselves, consciously trying to analyze what is going wrong and correct it. Tiger Woods, the great young golfer, does this all the time. If he feels his swing is a bit off during a round, he goes completely within himself and works to correct the problem. He does this even if he's winning by a good margin. He'll take practice swings between every shot, stopping the club at the top of the backswing or at the point of impact, to see if his body is properly aligned or if the angle of the club is correct. He often mutters to himself in the process. This constant, conscious awareness, analysis, and correction of small errors is one of the reasons Woods has developed arguably the best swing in golf—and why he has won so often.

Similarly, you need an awareness of your problem-solving process in order to acquire new heuristics and to learn how to become a better problem solver, in general. You also need to be aware of process when you get stuck so you can consult your repertoire of strategies and consciously select a new one. Process awareness is essential for breaking fixation and handling difficult strategic moments.

Process awareness is also essential because we tend to favor certain sets of heuristics based on our personalities. In fact, we often describe each other by our most often-employed strategies. "He is such a *planner*." "She is so *systematic*." "He is always *leaping in* before thinking." Each heuristic in a pair may require the adoption of a different attitude or emotion on the part of the problem solver in order to implement it. Take the heuristic pair of *leaping in* versus *holding back*, and think about how different people learn to use, say, a new remote control for a TV set. Some people leap in and start pushing buttons to discover what each button does. Others hold back and insist on reading the directions before attempting to use the remote. It takes an awareness of our natural process bias in order to consciously choose a different and perhaps uncomfortable approach.

### Externalization and the Need for a Common Language of Process

Finally, step four in this model of human problem solving deals with the importance of *externalization*, or thinking out loud. Externalization is the key to learning and teaching individual and group problem solving.

Think about a time when you learned from someone a new way of approaching a problem. This probably didn't happen just by watching someone work. Watching someone brilliantly think up a new solution to a problem that was stumping you just may have made you feel stupid. More likely, you experienced a key learning moment when someone "thought out loud" in front of you, sharing his or her strategies while working heuristically on a problem. That allowed you to observe the person's mind dancing around a problem, trying a particular strategy, seeing whether it worked, and then trying something different.

My best learning moments at design school occurred when professors came to my drawing table and, rather than just criticizing my work or suggesting a change, designed out loud in front of me. I could observe how their minds worked and how they implemented their strategies through drawing. They might have said something like, "Those two spaces look a bit awkward next to each other. How could we arrange them differently? Let's make a diagram of the main circulation flow. To do this, let's follow a first-time visitor to this building and ask ourselves which spaces we would want them to see, in what order." From this kind of dialogue, I learned about the power of *simplifying, diagramming,* and so forth. And the next time I was stumped I would ask myself, "How would the professor approach this problem?" I began to internalize the voices—and the problem-solving methods—of my professors.

If you don't have the words to describe an experience, it's often hard even to see or observe it. Without a mental framework, or what Neisser calls a cognitive structure, it's difficult to capture and retain related information. In the example of bird identification, having names for species and subspecies helps you distinguish and identify different birds and organize, retain, and access the information you learn about their songs, habitats, flight patterns, and so forth. In the same way, being able to attach a specific name or label to a heuristic strategy allows you to organize and access the information and experience you gather about its powers and limitations.

For example, let's take the pair of heuristic strategies I call *working forwards* and *working backwards*. Working forwards involves starting with what you know and building forwards, step-by-step—for example, writing a book by beginning with the introduction. The strategy of working backwards involves jumping to where you want to end up and building backwards—for example, writing the book's conclusion first, and then figuring out what chapters are needed to build to that conclusion. These two very powerful strategies can be applied in any situation. And you are much more likely to access and use each of these strategies if you learn a general, context-independent term to describe it. If, as so often happens in school, you were only exposed to these heuristics as part of a writing course, and the heuristics were never named, then you might be less likely to be able to apply them somewhere else, such as in a math class or a business situation. So, having a language and a vocabulary to describe various processes is very important for building your personal repertoire of problem-solving strategies.

## Relevance to Collaborative Problem Solving

Hopefully, this chapter has helped you understand more about how individuals solve problems and how you can become a more confident and effective problem solver. These concepts form the basis for everything that follows in this book and will be periodically mentioned again. Before we go on, however, let's look at the major lessons from this chapter and discuss how and why they relate to *collaborative* problem solving.

- **Problem solving is heuristic.** There is no one right way to solve problems. Likewise, there is no one right way to collaborate. At best, collaborative problem solving is an educated trial-and-error process. This is an important realization for groups that get mired in fighting over the right way to approach a problem. Group members must learn that it's more productive to simply select one problem-solving approach and see if it works. If it does not, they can try another. As we'll discuss in Chapter 5, it's the facilitator's job to help a group make conscious choices about which approaches to use in the course of a collaborative process. Thus, facilitators must have command of a whole tool kit of problem-solving strategies.

- **It's important to recognize strategic moments**. A group, like an individual, can get stuck and become fixated. The strategy it has been using just isn't working. The group needs to stop and make a conscious choice about what heuristic strategy it's going to use next. Again, it's the facilitator's responsibility to recognize these strategic moments and help the group make these important process decisions.

- **Problem-solving skills can be learned**. Just as with individuals, a group's problem-solving skill is dependent on the repertoire of problem-solving tools it knows how to use. A group can increase its ability to tackle difficult problems either by consciously acquiring new tools in formal training programs or through just-in-time learning, whereby the facilitator, or someone else in the group, suggests a new problem-solving process at the appropriate moment.

- **Having a common language of process is crucial**. In collaborative problem solving, it's absolutely essential that a group have a common language of process. For example, when a facilitator recommends that a group use the problem-solving method of brainstorming, everyone in the group must understand what brainstorming is and how it works. Effective collaborative problem solving requires members of a group to be able to communicate and agree on common processes, moment by moment. Likewise, an organization needs a common language of process to work effectively and collaboratively across organizational units. For example, we've found that without a common and clearly understood language for strategic planning, people in different parts of an organization will have different definitions for commonly used terms such as *goals, objectives, strategies,* and *tactics.* And if you are trying to build collaboration between organizations or within a community, all the stakeholders must agree on a language of process in order to be able to design a common way of working together.

*Solution to the anagram puzzle: "BETRAYAL."

# Part II

# The Principles of
# Collaboration

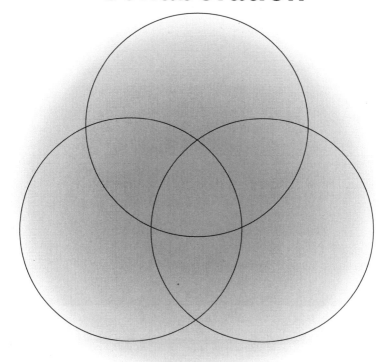

# Chapter 2

# Involve the Relevant Stakeholders

Over the past thirty years, my most interesting and challenging client has been my own company, Interaction Associates. At IA, we have consciously tried to implement the principles and values of collaborative action that we teach to clients, and to learn from both our failures and our successes. It's been a grand experiment.

Although I've been a board member since founding IA in 1969, I relinquished my day-to-day management responsibilities several years ago. Soon after that time, while still serving as chairman of the board, I became convinced that we needed to upgrade our computer systems to support collaboration and information sharing within the company. I also believed, for a variety of reasons, that we needed to reduce our dependency on Apple computers, even though I really preferred them.

As chairman, however, decisions about technology were not mine to make. They fell under the purview of the president. And so I faced a dilemma common to many managers and leaders today: I perceived a problem and even favored a particular solution, but I had no formal authority to make a unilateral decision.

Even if I had been president at the time, many people would probably have resisted or even sabotaged my efforts. I've always been a strong advocate for the adoption and use of new technology—so much so that I've generated some resistance, if not resentment, from my more technology-adverse colleagues. And as any IT manager will attest, if your internal customers don't support the implementation of a new system, your investment will be wasted and the technology underutilized. So, I knew this problem I perceived would have to be resolved using a collaborative approach. The question was, who needed to be involved in the collaboration?

Clearly, any consensus-based decision would have to be supported by the formal decision makers, specifically our president, our CFO, and the rest of the management team. The board of directors would need to approve the capital investment. The IT department had to be involved because they had the right expertise and would be responsible for implementing the new system. (I knew that some members of the department would probably be opposed to my proposal—in particular, one person who was a strong advocate for Apple technology and would have to be convinced that a cross-platform solution was required.) All of our internal departments and regional offices would have to come to understand how they would benefit from a new system, and be convinced that it was the highest and best use of our very limited capital. So, even though I was the founder and chairman of the company, I couldn't force this important decision. If any of these internal stakeholders were left out, and if there was not alignment and support throughout IA for this decision, inertia would set in, and it might be years before any significant investment in new technology would be made.

So, like anyone who wants to solve a problem collaboratively, I was faced with the immediate question: *Who* should be involved in the decision-making process and *how* should they be involved?

Perhaps you've already run up against this question in your efforts to collaborate with others in your organization or community. The fact is, there's a short answer and a long answer.

The short answer is this: *The power of collaboration comes from inclusion, not exclusion.* My experiences designing and facilitating collaborative processes over the years have taught me that this is true. And it's so fundamental to collaboration that I've made it the basis of the first principle: *Involve the relevant stakeholders.*

When the full range of differing interests and points of view is involved in solving a problem or making a decision, the solution is likely to be much more comprehensive and creative than if a small group of like-minded individuals acted on its own. The inclusion of all stakeholders also naturally creates a broader base of support for the solution and increases the likelihood that it will actually be implemented.

Of course, it's human nature to want to exclude those people who disagree with your ideas or who are difficult to work with. Stakeholder involvement requires a mindset of openness and inclusion, as well as trust in the process of collaboration. In any case, if you leave out an important stakeholder, your effort will be weakened or even doomed to fail from the start. If a key decision maker is not included, he or she may veto any decision that is reached. If you exclude people who really understand the problem and have relevant expertise, your conclusions may be flawed. And if you don't involve and win the support of those who will have to implement the solution, you may encounter insurmountable resistance.

So, that's the short answer.

The long answer is more complicated. The fact is, it's not always self-evident who the stakeholders are in a given situation and exactly how they should be involved. So, the remainder of this chapter provides the long answer. It will help you figure out who to involve in your next collaborative effort, and how to involve them.

## Who to Involve

A *stakeholder* is, quite simply, someone who has a stake in a given situation. A *stakeholder group* is a group of people (who may or may not be organized) who have the same interests or concerns regarding a situation. A stakeholder group might be, for instance, the employees of a certain department or homeowners in a particular neighborhood. There are four types of stakeholders:

1. Those with the formal power to make a decision

2. Those with the power to block a decision

3. Those affected by a decision

4. Those with relevant information or expertise

These categories are not mutually exclusive. For example, a formal decision maker may also have critical information and expertise. However, these classifications can be useful in helping you to figure out who to include in a problem-solving effort. The inclusion of individuals from each of the four categories adds to the strength of a collaborative effort. Let's consider each category separately.

### Those with Formal Power

The inclusion of formal decision makers—those people who are authorized to make final and binding decisions—gives teeth to a collaborative effort. The exclusion of such decision makers dooms a consensus-based decision to be no more than a recommendation that can then be ignored or dismissed. In the example discussed above, I didn't have the formal power to decide what new computer system to buy. So, I had to find a way to involve our president, the head of the IT department, and other key decision makers. The more you involve the managers who ultimately have to approve of a specific decision, the more strength and impact the collaborative effort will have.

If you aren't organizing a collaborative process but have been invited to participate in one, try to find out if the formal decision makers are personally involved. Are they treating the process seriously? How involved will they be? How much time and resources are they willing to commit to the effort? Do they see the collaborative process as an essential part of their planning, or is it simply window dressing to appease certain stakeholders? The answers to these questions are the litmus test for whether or not a collaborative process is "for real." If formal decision makers are included and if they are part of a final consensus, then they will probably return to their formal positions and act on the agreement. If they are left out, they may not, and the process will be greatly weakened.

But a collaborative process that includes only decision makers may also be flawed. Other types of stakeholders are critical, as well.

### Those with the Power to Block

The second type of stakeholders are those who are not formal decision makers but who can block or severely delay the implementation of a decision. Within an organization, these stakeholders may be managers or other employees whose methods of blocking may be very subtle: ignoring or not acting on a new policy, failing to inform others about it, or simply going through the motions of implementation. If these stakeholders are members of an organized union or interest group, they may have access to more adversarial methods, such as submitting a complaint, calling a strike, or filing a lawsuit. In any case, the impact of these blocking tactics can be significant, particularly in businesses in which rapid change is essential for economic survival.

In my situation at IA, the most obvious potential blocker was the vocal and persuasive supporter of Apple technology. But nearly everyone else at the company also could have fallen into this category, including managers in the regional offices who might have dragged their feet in implementing any decision, or busy employees who didn't see why they should bother to learn a new technology.

In the public arena in the United States and most other democracies, laws and regulations provide ample opportunities for concerned stakeholders to delay, if not block outright, the actions of a government agency or other organization. By using lawsuits, regulatory appeals, protests, or even media attention, for example, a determined interest group can tie up the implementation of a new policy or project for years, perhaps even making the costs of moving forward prohibitive. And in legislative bodies, the techniques for delay—such as the filibuster—are legendary.

So, if you want to organize a collaborative process—whether in the private or public sector—you should ask yourself: Who could block or delay the implementation of any decision that emerges from this process? Whose support do we need? Who could sabotage the effort? To the extent that you can involve these individuals or groups in some meaningful way, the process of collaborative action will be stronger. As I discuss in the next chapter, the effectiveness of a collaborative problem-solving process is measured not by how quickly you can *generate* a solution, but by how quickly you can *implement* it. The exclusion of potential blockers can severely threaten the implementation of any collaborative effort.

The mindset of inclusion can be difficult to maintain when you start to think about specific individuals you may need to involve in your collaborative process. It seems like there's always one person in every group, organization, or community who is considered important to the process but impossible to work with. Long ago, we at IA dubbed these types of individuals "alligators," since they are powerful but potentially disruptive. It is very tempting to try to exclude the alligators. It would be so much easier not to have to deal with them. But, truly, the process would be weaker for it. Excluding a powerful blocker can only make him or her more powerful—more able to claim with justification that the process was closed and unfair. To paraphrase an old saying, "It's better to have your enemy inside the tent spitting out, than outside the tent spitting in."

In our consulting work over the years, we have learned that alligators can become strong advocates for collaboration if they are treated with respect and educated about how to participate constructively. Often someone who is seen as difficult or disruptive has a concern or point of view that he or she feels the larger community has not heard or legitimized. Alligators are not passive or apathetic. They are vitally concerned about an issue and energetic in their advocacy. Unfortunately, the way they express their concerns and how they act in meetings often works against their interests. Their behaviors turn others off. If these people can learn how to work effectively within the guidelines and ground rules of a collaborative process, and if the other stakeholders can be encouraged to let go of their stereotyped preconceptions—to legitimize without necessarily agreeing with the concerns of the alligators—the whole situation can be reversed.

I had a memorable experience with an alligator back in the mid-1980s, during a citywide process in Newark, New Jersey, called the Newark Collaboration Group. At this time, Newark was plagued by high crime rates, poverty, racial tensions, and poor-quality schools, among many other problems. In addition, community leaders were often at odds. Those in the nonprofit social service fields felt that business leaders were not doing enough to invest in the community and provide jobs, while business executives felt that nonprofit leaders were ineffective and unable to deliver on their vision for the city. Trust in the city government was also low.

Newark was home to the headquarters of Prudential Financial, which was reconsidering its presence in the city. Prudential executives were concerned that they could not attract or keep high-quality talent; employees and prospective hires simply did not want to live in or near Newark. Executives had concerns about safety and wanted a better image for the city. Prudential had also invested a great deal in Newark real estate and in its social service infrastructure. So, before making any decisions about whether or not to leave, company officials decided they should work harder to reverse Newark's downward spiral, assess Newark's leadership and willingness to turn things around, and explore how a more collaborative, consensus-based planning process might help. IA was hired to convene and facilitate the process.

In the early phase of this collaborative effort, the primary alligator was the chief of police. He was trained as a lawyer and was highly skeptical of the ultimate effectiveness of the process, which was to include stakeholders from government, business, and the community. He just didn't think it would work, and he was very strident in voicing his concerns, to the point of being disruptive. But he kept showing up. When his concerns were finally acknowledged and he felt heard, he backed off and let the process go forward. By the time the group began to show some early success, the chief had accepted a new job in Washington, DC. But he was so supportive of the process at that point that he periodically flew back to Newark to attend critical meetings. This "alligator" had become one of the most vocal, constructive, and forceful advocates for the collaborative process. ·

Over the years, I've learned to love the alligators and disregard the negative comments made about them. To the best of my ability, I try to work with them, listen to their concerns, and help them learn how to turn their doubts into constructive feedback and their disruptive energy into positive action.

### Those Affected

The people who are potentially affected by a decision usually comprise the largest of the four categories of stakeholders. This category could include your whole organization or community, though often there are subsets of people who will be more affected and concerned than others. For example, in an organization that is revising its benefits package, decisions about maternity and paternity leave will be of more concern to employees who are considering having or adopting children than to employees who already have kids or who are past the child-rearing years. In a community dealing with rent stabilization, landlords and renters will clearly be more affected by the issue than others. In my situation at IA, I guessed that longer-term employees—who had been using the same computer system for years—might feel more affected by a system change than new employees. The fact is, the stakeholders most affected by a decision often have enough concern and commitment to migrate into the blocker category.

Clearly, every member of every affected stakeholder group can't always be involved in every face-to-face problem-solving meeting. Therefore, a collaborative process may need to rely on representatives of those stakeholder groups. It's essential to the effectiveness and credibility of a process that all points of view and interests be represented. The actual number of people who share each point of view (inside or outside the process) is less important. After all, the objective of a collaborative problem-solving process is to produce a solution that can satisfy the interests of all the stakeholder groups and deal with the root causes of the problem at hand to the greatest extent possible. If the underlying decision rule is consensus, any participant can block a proposed agreement. It doesn't matter if that person's point of view is shared by ten or one hundred other people; it carries the same weight in collaborative deliberations. (The dilemma of obstructionist behavior of one or more participants is handled by the threat of *fallback* to some form of win-lose decision making, as we'll see in the next chapter.) So, a party's interests will be safeguarded if there is someone involved who holds its stake or point of view. Each stakeholder group should be able to look at who is involved and feel that its interests are well represented and that its representatives are credible and sufficiently involved.

The challenge of representing all of the different points of view can be managed, in part, by asking one individual to speak for several different interests at one time. For example, an African-American woman from the accounting department in Boston could represent, if willing, African-American employees, female employees, members of the accounting department, and employees in the Boston office.

There are several reasons why the people affected by an issue should be tapped to help resolve it. For me, at its core, it's a matter of respect for human dignity. People who are directly affected by an issue deserve to be able to express their opinions about it and have a hand in formulating a solution. This concept undoubtedly developed out of the principle, so appreciated in democratic countries, of right to representation. But it's also a matter of practicality. If people feel they have been consulted and involved, they will be much more likely to support a decision, whether they agree with it or not. In fact, the workforce today increasingly demands and expects that important decisions will be addressed collaboratively. People want an opportunity to be involved. Moreover, the people closest to an issue are often the best ones to enlist in solving it. They live with the issue every day, have the most experience and information about it, and are often the most motivated to resolve it. And it is they who will have to support and implement any solution. It simply makes good sense to empower those closest to an issue to assume responsibility for resolving it.

### Those with Relevant Information or Expertise
In a collaborative process, the quality of the decisions is dependent on the quality of the expertise within the stakeholder group. Often, the inclusion of people from the first three categories of stakeholders (decision makers, blockers, and those affected) will guarantee that there is sufficient expertise to make informed decisions, but not always. It's important to ask if there is sufficient knowledge within the participant group to make a wise decision. What other expertise might be relevant? Who else could bring in valuable experience? Organizations and communities often have enough expertise resident within their own groups to address the issues they face.

It is sometimes necessary to bring in outside experts for both content and process. Unfortunately, however, organizations often outsource the entire problem to "experts." In these cases, the problem solving is done by consultants. Consequently, the real stakeholders are not engaged in or educated by the effort and thus have little connection to the experts' final recommendations. Inevitably, some disenfranchised stakeholder group ends up blocking the implementation of the consultants' proposals. And so, the solutions generated by the consultants sit on a shelf in a beautifully illustrated report, never to be acted upon.

In order to avoid this scenario, it's important that you first determine whether you need to bring in outside content expertise, process expertise, or both. If you need content expertise, the question to ask is: Do we need to have an expert work with us from the beginning, or is the expertise we need so specific that we can consult appropriate experts at the right time in the process? The answer to this question will vary from project to project. While outside expertise may seem expensive, keep in mind that a well-designed process can make the use of content consultants much more efficient, and therefore less costly. In the end, your group must either educate itself sufficiently about the subject at hand or reach out and include someone with the appropriate content expertise.

It's important to remember that many consultants are skilled in their own technical area (accounting, software development, e-business strategy, etc.), but they are not skilled at designing or facilitating collaborative processes. In fact, it's often a conflict of interest for someone to try to be both a process and a content expert. So you need to determine whether someone in your community has the credibility, skill, and willingness to serve as a process consultant and a facilitator. If you do not have someone who can fulfill that role, it's extremely important that at the beginning of your effort you contract someone from the outside to serve as a process expert. While content expertise may be optional, process design expertise and facilitation is not, as we will see in Chapters 4 and 5. Many individuals and firms now offer this kind of process expertise, so you'll have a wide variety of options to choose from.

So, to sum up this section: Power comes from inclusion, not exclusion. The more representatives of the four types of stakeholders you can include from the beginning in the collaborative planning process, the more power and impact the process will have.

## How to Involve Stakeholders

Once you have identified *who* your stakeholders are, you then face the question of *how* to involve them in a collaborative process. As I mentioned, it's often impossible for every stakeholder to be involved in face-to-face problem solving—particularly, say, in an organization of thousands of employees or a community of hundreds of thousands of citizens. In these cases, representatives of the main points of view can take part in a core problem-solving group. But that doesn't mean everyone else must just sit on the sidelines. In this section we will look at ways to involve *all* stakeholders in a collaborative problem-solving process. Specifically, I'll introduce the concept of *rings of involvement* and look at ways to extend involvement across time and place.

### Rings of Involvement

In designing a process of collaborative action, it's helpful to think in terms of four expanding rings of involvement, wherein each larger ring includes more people but at a decreased intensity of involvement. (See fig. 4.) Not all collaborative processes need to include all four rings.

The innermost ring is the core problem-solving group. The nature of this group depends on the number of potential stakeholders. When there are relatively few stakeholders—as in, say, a ten-person department in a company—then the core problem-solving group simply includes everyone. In a more complex collaborative process with hundreds or even thousands of stakeholders, the core group serves as a steering or executive committee. Typically, this committee is responsible for managing the process and integrating the work of the subcommittees. In an interorganizational or community process, this core problem-solving group usually has no formal decision-making power. Its power comes from the degree to which it is able to build a broad-based consensus among relevant stakeholder groups.

The second ring of involvement includes members of task forces

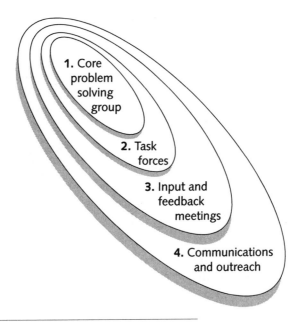

**Figure 4:**   Rings of involvement

or subcommittees. This ring still involves intensive problem solving, but the scope of the topic may be limited to a subset of the larger issue at hand. For example, a citywide planning effort might include task forces on affordable housing, small business, education, and parks and recreation. A corporate strategic planning process might include subcommittees on market segmentation and product offerings. In both cases, the stakeholders in each subcommittee would include those people who are most concerned and/or knowledgeable about the specific issue. The task force chairs might also be members of the executive or steering committee.

The third ring of involvement includes those people who might attend one or more large-group, "feed-forward" or feedback meetings. In feed-forward activities, the information flow proceeds from a few people out to many. For example, a committee may present progress reports or educational materials to a large set of interested parties. Feedback activities include focus groups, hearings, and brainstorming sessions, wherein people gather to offer ideas or reactions to the steering committee or a subcommittee. Thus, this third ring of involvement typically involves intense but periodic activity. Participants in this ring may turn up for a meeting and offer input, but they don't roll up their sleeves and engage in extended collaborative problem solving.

The outermost ring of involvement includes broad-based communications and outreach activities. Stakeholders involved in this ring may receive information through newsletters, e-mail, or the mass media. They may also offer some form of response from a distance (via ballot feedback, e-mail, or electronic polling). But they don't participate in face-to-face meetings. Through outreach efforts, large numbers of people can stay informed about a problem-solving process without making much of a commitment in time or resources.

In setting up a collaborative process and inviting people to become involved, it's important to remember that a stakeholder can do more damage to a process by being left out than by being included. Often, if you extend an invitation to someone with an explanation of the time commitments required, the individual will feel acknowledged but opt for a less-intense ring of involvement. If you exclude that person, however, he or she may come pounding at the door.

It's also essential to keep the boundaries between the four rings of involvement permeable. During the course of a collaborative effort, individuals may become more interested and committed to the effort or, conversely, they may lose interest, become burned out, or get pulled away by other commitments. The process must allow for these adjustments. If participants feel they cannot become more involved if they want to—if they feel locked into a particular ring of involvement—they may challenge the inclusiveness (and therefore the legitimacy) of the process. Although it's not ideal to disrupt the work of a task force by constantly adding new members, groups have to resist the tendency to bond and close their doors to outsiders. Sometimes an important and motivated stakeholder surfaces after a process is well under way. It's more important to offer a way to include this person than to argue that it's too late to get involved.

The fourth ring of involvement (outreach and communications) is particularly important in this regard because it allows people to learn about the process and move up the rings of involvement if they desire. Collaboration can't be open and inclusive if it is invisible to the larger organization or community. If people don't know a planning effort is happening, they won't have an opportunity to volunteer or know how to monitor and participate in the outer rings of involvement. Even with the best intentions of the sponsors, if a collaborative process is not well publicized, it may be perceived as closed and exclusive.

It's the responsibility of the stakeholder representatives to keep their constituencies involved through periodic reports and efforts to solicit input and reaction. If the stakeholders aren't kept informed, they won't have an opportunity to give input and support their representatives in the effort. Visibility and transparency contribute to openness, which, in turn, ensures maximum appropriate involvement—all of which increases the power and impact of collaborative action.

### Extending Involvement across Time and Place

It is now possible to collaborate across time and place through the use of various collaboration technologies, sometimes called *groupware*. These technologies allow for much larger numbers of people to become involved in collaborative processes, both face-to-face and virtually.

I first caught a glimpse of the exciting potential of technology to enhance collaboration in 1968, during a presentation at the fall Joint Computer Conference in San Francisco. At this time, computer technology was really in its infancy. The presentation was given by Doug Englebart, a wise, kindly computer scientist who was then leading an exciting project at the Stanford Research

Institute called the Augmented Human Intellect Research Center. He had assembled an energetic, brilliant, and diverse group of electrical engineers, software developers, psychologists, and sociologists to study how a group of people could augment their creativity, productivity, and collaboration through the use of computer technology.

At this conference, Doug sat in front of a spellbound audience, effortlessly manipulating text information on a black-on-white computer display (most displays were still white-on-black), using a pointing device in his right hand (soon to become known as a "mouse") and typing commands on a five-fingered device in his left hand (an instrument that never became popular). All of Doug's actions—as well as the activities of his colleague in Palo Alto—were visible to the audience on large video screens. Doug and the rest of his colleagues were creating a common set of easily accessible records and data, a first important milestone in the field of computer-supported work. Doug was able to collapse, expand, and view the information in many different ways, as well as link an item in one file to an item in a different file and jump backwards and forwards between them. What we were seeing, it turned out, were the origins of the hypertext language and the Web.

To understand the promise of these tools today, it's helpful to think about collaboration in terms of the four quadrants in Figure 5.

The same time/same place quadrant includes those technologies designed to support face-to-face meetings. These technologies are often referred to as *electronic meeting systems* or EMSs. Some of these tools make it possible for large numbers of people to participate in a meeting simultaneously and brainstorm or comment at the same time through the use of networked computer terminals. I will discuss some of the general advantages and limitations of EMSs in Chapters 5 and 6, which have to do with facilitation and group memory.

The same time/different place quadrant includes the familiar technologies of telephone and video conferencing. It also includes software programs that allow participants to share documents and

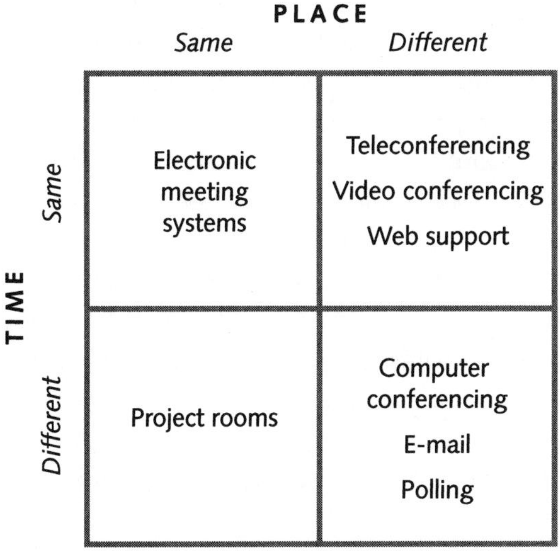

**PLACE**

|  | | Same | Different |
|---|---|---|---|
| **TIME** | *Same* | Electronic meeting systems | Teleconferencing<br>Video conferencing<br>Web support |
| | *Different* | Project rooms | Computer conferencing<br>E-mail<br>Polling |

**Figure 5:** Collaboration over time and place

*Source: Institute for the Future, adapted from "Time/Place Matrix," Groupware: Computer Support for Business Teams, Bob Johansen, 1998.*

presentations in real time. Such software has been greatly improved in recent years, and is now more effective and cost-effective than ever. When used in conjunction with a Web connection, it makes it possible for stakeholders around the world to view and manipulate the same document simultaneously. Presentations and training sessions with graphics and sound can be given to large numbers of people, with feedback and questions handled by telephone or computer. Global companies have for some time been using these technologies to communicate with all of their employees at once.

In the public sector, many communities have experimented with a low-tech version of same time/different place collaboration. In these cases, local radio and TV programs have been coupled with discussion groups and telephone polling as a way to involve citizens in planning processes.

The different time/different place quadrant includes voice mail and e-mail, as well as computer conferencing and other software programs that create virtual meeting places. These tools allow large numbers of people to participate whenever and wherever they want to. Most systems keep track of the last time a participant visited the virtual discussion and display comments and entries that he or she has not yet seen. These groupware tools have enabled some remarkable collaborations. My father, for example, an early adopter of computer conferencing, has hosted online discussions on a variety of heated topics (such as abortion rights), and has participated in a virtual support group that rarely gets together face-to-face but has continued online for more than ten years, with members supporting each other through illnesses and other major life transitions.

In another sort of different time/different place collaboration, companies including Motorola and Cisco have formed project teams in which different functional units are located in different time zones. When the U.S.-based engineers have finished their work day, they might send their requests and questions to their India-based programming team members who, in turn, e-mail their responses and their own questions back to the United States by the next morning.

Strangely enough, the final quadrant—different time/same place collaboration—is the least developed, even though it doesn't require sophisticated technology. It includes processes in which people collaborate in some way by visiting the same place at different times. In a sense, museums and libraries support this kind of involvement. At those institutions, large numbers of people pass through the same place at different times to learn and potentially to contribute. Some collaborative efforts have created project rooms in which interested stakeholders can drop by to view process maps and progress reports and leave comments in suggestion boxes.

If you are designing a process of collaborative problem solving, you will need to make conscious choices about which ring of involvement is appropriate for each stakeholder and which group-ware technology to use. Does the individual or group want to be involved in face-to-face meetings, or could participation be handled virtually using a technology from one of the other quadrants? If the latter, what specific groupware tool is the most available, easy to use, and cost-effective?

The development of new computer technologies and high-speed networks has paralleled and further enabled the growing demand for collaboration. One of the great drivers of productivity in the United States is the advances in technology that allow anybody in an organization to have instantaneous access to vast amounts of shared information and to communicate and collaborate with anyone else in the organization, or, in fact, almost anyone in the world. These technologies have removed the need for middle management to control the flow of information (in fact, it's now almost impossible for anyone to control the flow) and have supported the creation of flatter, more networked, and more collaborative organizations.

## Conclusion

So there you have it—the first principle of collaborative action: Involve the relevant stakeholders. Such a simple idea, but so powerful. Together with the next idea, consensus, it creates a foundation for the rest of the principles of collaboration. David Chrislip and Carl Larson (1994) capture the concept in what they refer to as the "collaborative premise." They write: "If you bring the appropriate people together in constructive ways with good information, they will create authentic visions and strategies for addressing the shared concerns of the organization or community."

I couldn't agree more. The power of collaborative action comes from inclusion, not exclusion. The process must be open and inclusive. If the relevant stakeholders can be involved appropriately and if they can reach consensus, the solution is likely to be of higher quality and more easily implemented than if it were created and enforced by one person alone.

The belief underlying this principle is that well-intentioned people can work together to find win-win solutions to challenging issues. It's a matter of basic respect for human dignity—a belief that people have the right to be involved in decisions that affect their lives.

To design an effective collaborative process, then, you must identify the four types of stakeholders and offer them the opportunity to participate in one of the rings of involvement, from face-to-face meetings to virtual participation through the use of groupware technologies. The credibility and power of a process of collaborative action depends, in large part, on the effective involvement of these stakeholders.

# Chapter 3

# Build Consensus Phase by Phase

Bob, the manager of a large car dealership, assembled his sales team to discuss a pressing issue. "We've got a problem," he began. "I've noticed a drop in the sales of our station wagons over the past two months. I'm convinced that the cause of the problem is that new foreign dealership down the street. If we want to hold on to our customer base, we need to drop the price of our wagons immediately. So, I propose that beginning next week we reduce the price of all our station wagons by $2,000. This will cut into your commissions, so I'd like your support for this action. Do you all agree with my plan?"

Bob's statement was met, at first, with stunned silence. Finally, several salespeople spoke up. One person questioned whether sales have really dropped so much. Another wondered whether the problem really was the new foreign dealership. And a third thought $2,000 was too big of a price reduction. Quickly, the meeting devolved into a series of arguments over this wide variety of topics.

Now, Bob is a hypothetical character, but I see his approach to "collaboration" attempted all the time in the real world. Bob thought he could build consensus collaboratively by getting all the key stakeholders in a room together and persuading them to support his ideas. He quickly learned that consensus building doesn't work that way. It's not possible to simply throw people in a room and assume consensus will emerge if you push hard enough. And proposing a solution at the outset of a collaborative process, as Bob did, typically only divides a group and heightens the conflict.

This chapter aims to help you understand how consensus building *really* works, and to avoid the kind of disaster Bob experienced. Like stakeholder involvement, consensus building is fundamental to all the remaining chapters in this book. Collaboration means working together; working together involves making agreements; and one powerful way to make agreements is to work for consensus. As I will discuss in Chapter 7 (on facilitative leadership), a leader can be collaborative without always trying to reach consensus, but consensus on a win-win solution is usually the best possible outcome. To grasp the idea of consensus, let's examine four aspects of it:

1. The definition and benefits of consensus

2. How consensus is built

3. The differences between facilitated, collaborative problem solving and mediated negotiation

4. What happens if you can't reach consensus

## The Definition and Benefits of Consensus

A group reaches *consensus* on a decision when every member can agree to support that decision. Each person may not think it's the very best decision, but he or she can buy into it and actively support its implementation. No one in the group feels that his or her fundamental interests have been compromised. Consensus is not "almost everybody." It's unanimous support for a decision, in the same way that a jury returns a unanimous verdict.

The concept of consensus building is particularly powerful because it connects with both our minds and our hearts. It speaks to both what is possible and what is right—what makes practical sense and what is the moral thing to do. The rational argument in favor of consensus building is that consensus building produces a higher-quality decision than other decision-making processes. For example, a decision made by consensus will tend to be better than one made by a majority vote. A number of research studies have shown that if a group adopts some basic collaborative ground rules—like working diligently for consensus and avoiding voting—the quality of its decisions will be higher than if a group resorts to voting too quickly (i.e., Michaelsen, et al., 1989, and Herbert & Yost, 1979). Moreover, most of the time, a decision forged by consensus will be better than one made by any of the members on his or her own. The struggle to satisfy and incorporate the views of all members tends to produce a synergy and a creativity not possible when members work alone. Also, if all the key stakeholders are involved in forging the consensus, they will make a decision that they agree to implement, so it's a workable solution. Moreover, consensus is nearly always attainable. It is possible most of the time (in my experience, at least three out of four times) for a group of individuals to reach a consensus decision.

But even setting the rational arguments aside, my heart has always told me that consensus building is the right thing to do. Stakeholders have a right to be involved in decisions that affect them, and they each have great value to add to the process. Consensus building respects the intelligence and dignity of all individuals. And, when treated with respect and dignity, most people will act rationally and can bring important insights to a collaborative effort. Wouldn't you want to have a say in a decision that affects your life? Don't you feel that others deserve that opportunity, as well?

So, the promise of building consensus in our organizations and communities speaks to both our minds and hearts. It provides us with a vision of how things should be, a direction to head in, a goal to achieve. It's hard to argue with. Who wouldn't want the kind of alignment and support that consensus offers? The problem is how to do it.

## How Consensus Is Built

As Bob discovered, you can't reach consensus by pushing for a favorite solution from the outset and hoping others will eventually acquiesce. When Bob did this, it immediately became clear that some people not only disagreed with his proposed solution, they also questioned his analysis of the problem. Bob learned the hard way the second principle of collaboration: *Build consensus phase by phase.* You can't reach consensus by going for it directly; you have to work up to it gradually.

The process of building small agreements one at a time begins the first time stakeholders get together. The first agreements should be about process (e.g., ground rules, agendas, roles, desired outcomes, time frame). Once a group reaches agreement about how it's going to work together, it can move on to the substantive issues at hand. When discussing the content of an issue, a group should generally begin by perceiving, defining, and analyzing the problem (or by *visioning,* as we will discuss in the next chapter) before entertaining alternatives and solutions. So, a corollary to the second principle is: *If a you can't agree on the problem, you won't agree on the solution.*

In 1969, after studying the literature on problem solving and creativity and doing a bit of experimenting, I settled on the following six-phase model of problem solving, each phase of which addresses a different objective or task. We still use this model regularly at Interaction Associates.

**Phase 1.    Perception**: Is there a problem? How do you feel about it? Is it legitimate to discuss the problem openly?

**Phase 2.    Definition**: What is the problem? What are its limits or boundaries?

**Phase 3.    Analysis**: Why does the problem exist? What are its causes?

**Phase 4.    Generation of Alternatives**: What are some possible solutions to the problem?

**Phase 5.    Evaluation**: What criteria must a good solution meet? Which alternatives are better or more acceptable than others?

**Phase 6.    Decision Making**: Which solution can we agree on? Which alternative can we commit to implementing?

*(See the Resources section for a simplified version of the last three phases.)*

To build consensus, then, a group must make agreements one phase at a time. For example, a group needs to agree that it's even legitimate to discuss an issue before it can agree on a definition of the problem. In some organizations and communities, certain problems are treated as undiscussable—usually because if they are publicly recognized, leaders would feel responsible for solving them, and they think they don't have any answers.

I saw a dramatic example of this phenomenon when working with a manager and his direct reports at a district office of the Social Security Administration. The office was located in a relatively poor section of the San Francisco Bay Area. The staff, mostly women, were responsible for handing out welfare checks, which, because of processing problems, were being delayed. Every day, these women were being threatened by angry people demanding their checks and were afraid for their safety. Their manager, however, didn't want to acknowledge the problem because he didn't know how to solve it. During a meeting I facilitated with the manager and his team, he came to understand that he could legitimize the problem and acknowledge the fear that his staff felt without having to assume total responsibility for alleviating the situation. The staff was very relieved to finally be able to talk openly about their daily experiences. In the course of the meeting, they worked collaboratively with the manager to develop several solutions that would improve their situation in the short term, while the larger problem of speeding up the check processing was being resolved.

Problem perception is just the first phase in the problem-solving model. This phase, along with the next two phases—definition and analysis—focus on the issue at hand. They make up what we call the *problem space*. The last three phases—the generation of alternatives, evaluation, and decision making—focus on how to resolve the issue. They make up the *solution space*.

There is a powerful relationship between the problem space and the solution space. How a group defines a problem has a significant impact on the range of solutions it considers. A management team that defines its problem as "how to get invoices to clients within thirty days of completion of work," for example, will develop a different set of solutions than if the problem were defined as "how to fire our bookkeeper."

The bulk of the work of consensus building takes place in the problem space. Often when the group has reached consensus on the definition of a problem, the solutions will almost "fall out." By contrast, if group members jump to the solution space too quickly, each may feel impelled to advocate strongly for his or her position, thereby polarizing the group. This is one of the reasons why *Robert's Rules of Order*, which outlines standard parliamentary procedure for meetings, is such an ineffective method for building consensus. It begins in solution space by requiring a participant to "make a motion"—to propose a solution. The motion is debated before the group even agrees what problem is being addressed.

Because problem solving is a heuristic, trial-and-error process, there will be some natural jumping back and forth between phases. For example, sometimes a stakeholder will feel so strongly about a particular solution that it makes sense to jump to the solution space early on, have the person present the alternative, have other group members ask clarifying questions, and then defer evaluation and return to the problem space for further analysis and problem definition. But the key is this: *Effective collaborative problem solving requires that the whole group stay focused and together in the same phase of problem solving.* If one person wants to go back to problem definition, the whole group must consciously go back with him or her. If a group tries to, say, generate solutions and evaluate them at the same time, participation will probably shut down. People aren't likely to offer up possible solutions after they hear their colleagues' ideas getting shot down. It's essential that everyone has a chance to contribute before ideas are critiqued. The group should stay in the phase of alternative generation until its collective creativity has been fully mined.

What makes group problem solving even more complicated is that each phase of problem solving is, itself, a problem to be solved. In order to move forward, for example, a group needs to reach consensus on the definition of the problem. In order to do this, the group may have to generate alternative definitions, evaluate them, and make a decision about which definition they are going to use. Within each phase, then, some or all of the other phases may be employed. So the statement above needs to be amended to read: *Effective collaborative problem solving requires that the whole group stay focused and together in the same phase and sub-phase of problem solving.*

Furthermore, many different heuristic strategies and problem-solving methods exist, as discussed in Chapter 1. And, as we have also seen, there is no one right way to approach a problem. A group often has to try a number of different strategies before making headway. So the above statement needs to be further modified to read: *Effective collaborative problem solving requires that the whole group stay focused and together in the same phase and sub-phase of problem solving and using the same problem-solving method.*

We've also found that effective consensus building involves making lots of little conditional agreements at the conclusion of each phase of problem solving. A facilitator may ask, for example, "Is anyone *not* able to live with this definition of the problem? OK, so we can move on to possible solutions? Remember, we can always come back and redefine the problem if we need to." These little agreements build a foundation for consensus in the final phase of decision making. While the decision-making phase sometimes requires trade-offs and negotiation, this foundation of agreements helps to create a spirit of goodwill and the common understanding that consensus is possible.

The agreements also serve like pitons for a mountaineer. If one agreement pulls out, the rest will keep the group from falling back too far. Sometimes when a group is divided between two or more alternatives, it may be necessary to return to an earlier phase to broaden the solution space. With a little extra work, an even better, more creative alternative may be found. It is this heuristic flexibility that makes consensus building possible and so effective. If a group has done a good job of building agreements phase by phase, the last phase of decision making is often the easiest. Consensus just seems to emerge.

## Facilitated, Collaborative Problem Solving vs. Mediated Negotiation

There are two basic approaches to building consensus among multiple stakeholders: (1) facilitated, collaborative problem solving (which we've been discussing here) and (2) mediated negotiation. For the sake of simplicity, I'll sometimes refer to these two approaches as "facilitation" and "mediation," respectively.

In 1970, when my exploration of problem-solving processes led me into the field of conflict resolution, the commonly accepted approach to building agreement between two or more parties in the public sector was mediation, a process that had arisen out of settlement practices in labor-management disputes. To oversimplify somewhat, in a formal mediated negotiation in the public sector, the different stakeholders were organized into negotiation teams with official representatives. For example, for a dispute about where a new power plant should be built, the parties might be organized into power companies, government regulators, ratepayers, local governments, and environmental organizations. The mediator would meet with these representatives, individually or in caucus with those they represented—to explore interests, offer suggestions (sometimes in the form of a *single negotiating text*—a draft, proposed agreement), and challenge entrenched positions. The mediator would also engage in shuttle diplomacy and be actively involved in shaping the content of the evolving agreement.

By contrast, facilitated, collaborative problem solving involves bringing all parties together face-to-face in a meeting or series of meetings. With the help of a facilitator (someone focused solely on the problem-solving process), the stakeholders work together to build agreement step by step. In 1970, the idea of building consensus with all of the parties meeting face-to-face seemed to many old-time mediators as unmanageable and potentially explosive.

Since then, the lines between these two philosophies have blurred considerably. Most practitioners draw concepts and techniques from both approaches, and many use the terms *mediator* and *facilitator* interchangeably. However, for this discussion it's useful to heighten the distinctions between mediated negotiation and facilitated collaborative problem solving in order to understand the different underlying mental models involved. While the end result of both approaches is an agreement made by consensus, the process involved is quite different, as are the lasting effects on the relationships between the parties. We'll look at five key differences between the two processes: the creation of doubt; the objectives of the process; the organization of stakeholders; the role and mindset of the process leader; and the relative ease of initiation.

## The Creation of Doubt

The first key difference involves a useful concept in negotiation theory called the *creation of doubt*. As a party involved in a dispute, you will not be likely to change your negotiating position unless you doubt that your offer will be acceptable to the other party. If you are convinced that the other side will agree to your offer, why should you change it? In mediated negotiation, where the mediator is primarily working with the parties in caucus, the mediator must be the agent for the creation of doubt. In other words, he or she must diplomatically challenge the beliefs or position of each party in order to promote movement toward an agreement. "Do you really think that the other party will accept this offer?" a mediator might ask. "Is winning on this point essential to your basic interests? What could you offer in return?"

In collaborative problem solving, by contrast, the facilitator need not play this role. Since the parties are facing each other in the same room, they will raise doubts and challenge each others' positions naturally. If anything, the facilitator must slow down these challenges and make sure they are made in a constructive way, thereby helping everyone to listen to and understand each others' underlying interests rather than overreact to the specifics of a proposal.

## Objectives of the Process

The overall objectives of mediation and facilitation are also somewhat different. To be sure, both mediation and facilitation seek to reach consensus. But mediation often doesn't go much beyond that—it's singularly focused on getting results. Facilitated collaborative problem-solving, on the other hand, tends to also focus on improving both the long-term relationships among the parties and the parties' problem-solving skills.

Let's look at the relationships aspect first. Where there are a limited number of highly polarized parties who don't intend to work together again and who just want a resolution to a dispute, then mediation may be the best, and in some cases, the only, approach available. But where the parties must continue to work or live together, or where the conflict in question has happened before and is likely to recur, then the goal may not be just to reach an agreement on a specific issue, but also to improve communications and understanding and to build the capacity for avoiding conflict in the future. Success may be defined not only in terms of getting results, but also in terms of improving the processes and relationships of the stakeholders. In cases like this, keeping the parties separate and having a mediator assume responsibility for forging a resolution may not be helpful. Facilitative, face-to-face problem solving may be much more effective.

For example, if two spouses are so angry with one another and polarized in their positions that all they want is a divorce settlement, mediation may be the best approach to dispute resolution, short of going to court. But if the two people still love each other and are facing an issue that is driving them apart (e.g., whether or not to move, buy a house, or have another child), then it may be more fruitful to resolve the problem face-to-face with a facilitating third party, thereby enabling them to learn to listen and collaborate more effectively.

I first saw how face-to-face, facilitated consensus building can help rebuild relationships and forge trust while working on a new approach to neighborhood dispute resolution. In 1975, my friend Tom Layton, executive director of the Gerbode Foundation, introduced me to a young lawyer named Ray Shonholtz. It turned out that all of us had offices in the same old warehouse south of Mission Street in San Francisco. Ray was concerned by the number of neighbor-to-neighbor disputes that were clogging the local courts—conflicts that shouldn't have been there in the first place. Often the issues were minor: barking dogs, loud music, trash in the stairwells. What was needed was communication between the parties and a restoration of relationships—relationships that were deteriorating and becoming polarized as the issues lingered in the courthouse.

Ray had been impressed by community dispute resolution processes being used in China, Cuba, and Scotland, in which disputes were resolved by community members themselves. While the models would not work in American society without significant modification, Ray was intrigued by the self-help approach to neighborhood dispute resolution and the power and force of peer pressure. He saw that if a dispute was heard and resolved in front of the parties' neighbors, those neighbors could exert pressure to hold the disputants to their agreements. Most of the time, lawyers and police didn't need to get involved. Ray wanted to see if a neighborhood dispute resolution model could be developed for the United States as an alternative to employing the criminal justice system for minor community issues.

During the next few years, I worked with Ray and his colleagues at his new nonprofit organization, the Community Board Program, to develop and test a simple four-phase dispute resolution model. In this model, trained community members facilitated face-to-face, collaborative processes that were witnessed by other concerned citizens. The model involved four basic steps:

1. Allowing each party to present his or her concerns to the panel of trained community members

2. Enabling the parties to listen to each other, understand each other's interests, and acknowledge their own roles in the initial dispute and in the continuation of the conflict

3. Engaging in joint problem solving to generate potential solutions to the conflict

4. Forging a final agreement

The Community Board Program is still going strong today. It maintains a roster of about three hundred trained volunteers who handle a wide range of community and neighborhood disputes.

This story illustrates another difference in objective between mediation (as traditionally practiced) and facilitation—the latter seeks to transfer collaborative capabilities to the participants.

Participants in a facilitated, collaborative effort often learn a great deal about the processes of collaborative problem solving and consensus building simply by experiencing it first hand, and they can apply this learning elsewhere in their work and home lives. If the process is successful, they learn that collaboration and consensus are possible—often on difficult issues about which the participants never thought a win-win solution could be fashioned. And a good facilitator is constantly educating the group by offering little "commercials" about such things as the heuristic nature of problem solving, the phases of problem solving, the principles of collaboration, and so forth. As a process of collaboration proceeds, participants may learn to be more facilitative, thereby making the group as a whole more effective.

### The Organization of Stakeholders

A third important difference between mediated negotiation and facilitated collaborative problem solving is the way in which stakeholders are organized to participate. In a case involving many different interest groups or parties, a mediated approach requires the stakeholders to organize into a very limited number of negotiating teams, and to choose representatives. This is done to simplify negotiations, as much for the sake of the mediator as anything else. So in a public-sector dispute, for example, stakeholders might find themselves in one of three teams: government, private sector, or community. The assumption is that members of each team would share a significant degree of alignment in their points of view and interests.

A facilitated approach does not impose this limitation. Each stakeholder can participate directly (through one of the several rings of involvement) and speak for himself or herself. One environmental group does not need to share the same point of view as another.

What I've learned over the years is that in the process of collaborative action, strange alliances sometimes emerge between assumed adversaries. Stakeholders may join hands across the table and find themselves working supportively with those they perceived as enemies. For example, on a specific issue or sub-problem, a for-profit firm may share the same point of view as a community group. The flexibility, openness, and inclusiveness of the collaborative process promotes these kinds of alliances and works for the development of an inclusive "we" attitude as opposed to an "us vs. them" mentality.

### Role and Mindset of the Process Leader

The fourth distinction between mediation and facilitation lies in the role and mindset of the group process leader. I will cover in some depth in Chapter 5 the powerful idea of the facilitator. And I should acknowledge here again that most practitioners combine elements of both processes. But, in general, mediators tend to work with organized parties, often in caucus, and are actively involved in formulating the content of an agreement, while facilitators play more of a pure process role and work primarily with all of the stakeholders in the same room. Also, mediators tend to view stakeholders more as adversaries who will negotiate but not collaborate in the development of win-win solutions. Facilitators, by contrast, tend to believe that with a modest amount of goodwill and the right structure and process, stakeholders can work together constructively to build agreements. The underlying mindset is a belief in the capability and creativity of human beings and the power of collaborative action.

It has been demonstrated in several different fields that the attitude and mind-set of the professional has a significant impact on how the clients behave. If a teacher believes in the potential of her students, the students tend to perform better than if they are perceived as difficult and low potential. So, too, if a third party believes that stakeholders can collaboratively create solutions to their problems, then that's what, in my experience, tends to happen.

The role of facilitator is often more acceptable and less threatening to stakeholders than the role of mediator, especially in the private sector. With facilitation, the ultimate control of the process is firmly in the hands of the participants, and the facilitator does not need to be an expert in the content of the issue. Therefore, participants are less likely to feel that they are abdicating their responsibility. For example, if two managers in a company are in conflict, they will probably more readily agree to a facilitated meeting in which they will try to work out their differences face-to-face than to a mediated negotiation in which an internal or external mediator would serve as a shuttle diplomat and to try to fashion an agreement.

During the 1970s, a number of federal agencies in the United States, including the Bureau of Land Management (BLM) and the U.S. Forest Service, became very interested in nonadversarial approaches to conflict resolution. Both the BLM and the Forest Service were confronting large-scale environmental disputes and realized that their field managers needed new tools for resolving these issues. The two agencies were actively exploring the advantages and disadvantages of mediated and facilitated processes of multiparty conflict resolution. I co-led a number of workshops in which land managers could experience, in a role-playing situation, what it was like to participate in *both* types of processes.

Participants discovered that when they were in caucus trying to agree on their negotiating position and what they wanted to demand of the other party, they found themselves getting more polarized and adversarial. They easily projected negative feelings and positions onto the "other side," and got more strident in their demands. However, when the "other side" was in the same room, where perceptions could be checked out directly and reactions experienced firsthand, they found it was much harder to demonize the other parties or make unreasonable demands. These managers found that there was a significant difference in the look and feel of the process when they were sitting across the table from the other party and negotiating, as opposed to when they were working side by side, collaborating on a mutually acceptable solution.

## Ease of Initiation

One final point about the benefits of facilitation, as compared to mediation: What makes facilitated collaboration so appealing and so useful is that it's easy to initiate. The risks and pre-conditions of a facilitated, consensus-building process are initially quite low. The necessary conditions are quite simple. The participants must be able to agree to:

- come together in one place (physical or virtual);

- explore without commitment how everyone might be able to work together collaboratively;

- accept that the other participants have a right to be involved in the initial exploration; and

- abide by ground rules once they have been agreed to.

Participants may come to the process with animosity and distrust about whether anything constructive will happen. But they only have to agree to try collaborating for one meeting, usually only dealing with process design issues. The parties do not have to give up any of their fallback options. The process can be aborted at any time. There is very little down side.

## What Happens if You Can't Reach Consensus

When a group is seeking consensus, it's essential that it specify a fallback decision-making rule, in case consensus can't be reached. After all, there will be times when a win-win solution can't be found, and the organization or community must be able to make a decision and move forward. The fallback is generally a traditional win-lose decision-making method. In an organizational setting, the method will differ depending on the type of organization, be it a *hierarchy* or a *horizontal, representational body*. In a community setting, the fallback concept is more complex.

### Fallback in Hierarchies and Horizontal Organizations

A hierarchy, of course, is a simple, clear structure for clarifying the delegation of authority and responsibility to specific individuals. It is pyramidal in nature, consisting of a single person at the top and broadening out to numerous levels and branches below. In a hierarchy, everyone is responsible *for* the actions of those below them, and responsible *to* the individual directly above them. Decisions and responsibilities flow clearly upward and downward. It may seem that traditional hierarchies are long gone, given the large number of team-based organizations and virtual corporations in existence today. And it's true that many organizational structures today look more like spider webs or networks (with multiple reporting relationships) than simple hierarchies. But the underlying mental model in these organizations is still that of hierarchy, with final decision-making authority delegated to specific individuals. This is true in corporations, nonprofit organizations, and government agencies alike.

As a leader or manager in a hierarchical organization, you can delegate a decision but you can't abdicate your ultimate responsibility or authority. You can't assemble your direct reports and then allow yourself to be outvoted. But you can organize an informal group to solve a problem collaboratively—using a consensus decision rule—as long as the fallback is that you, the formal decision maker, have the final say.

For example, let's say you're a manager with five people reporting directly to you. The formal structure, when everyone is working by themselves in their offices, might be diagrammed like the left side of Figure 6. You have the formal authority to make or approve all decisions that relate to those who report to you. You can't abdicate this responsibility. But you can convene your direct reports for an informally structured consensus-based meeting and seek a win-win solution to an issue, as shown on the right side of the figure. If consensus can be achieved (and you must be part of this consensus) you can return to your formal position of authority and act on the consensus decision. If consensus can't be reached,

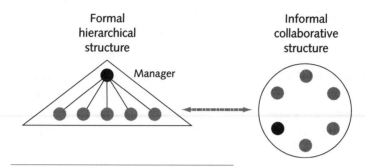

**Figure 6:** Fallback in a hierarchical organization

the fallback is that you, as senior manager, make the call. You can't be outvoted. It's important that all participants in the consensus-building effort understand that you are the fallback.

With this notion of fallback, a formal hierarchy can coexist with and take advantage of the power and inclusiveness of consensus building. Members of a hierarchical organization can periodically convene under the decision-making rules of an informal, collaborative structure to search for consensus, while preserving the final, fallback decision-making authority.

A similar type of parallel process can take place in horizontal, representative bodies (e.g., boards of directors, commissions, elected legislatures). In these organizations, the decision-making process is voting, and the decision rule is usually a majority vote of a quorum of members. Typically, in fact, these decision-making processes are guided by formal parliamentary procedures, such as those outlined in *Robert's Rules of Order*. But horizontal organizations don't have to operate that way. They can and should convene in more informal, collaborative, consensus-based structures to seek win-win solutions by consensus before resorting to voting. There's a formal parliamentary mechanism for doing so, actually—it's called "moving into a committee of the whole." (America's first Continental Congress moved into a committee of

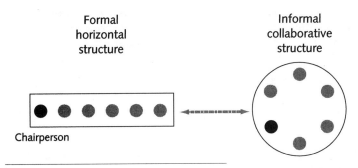

**Figure 7:** Fallback in a horizontal organization

the whole in order to have more free-flowing discussion and ultimately to reach consensus on the Declaration of Independence.) Once a consensus agreement is reached, the organization can resume using its traditional procedures and vote to ratify any decision that is made. If no consensus is reached, the fallback is the traditional voting procedure. The movement between formal and informal structures in a horizontal organization is diagrammed in Figure 7.

Again, in both hierarchical and horizontal structures, the power of informal, collaborative problem-solving sessions derives from the inclusion of key decision makers. Simply put: If the formal decision makers are included, and if they are part of a final consensus, then they will be likely to return to their formal positions and act on the agreement. If they are left out, the process will be greatly weakened.

### Fallback in Multi-Organization Collaborations

When multiple organizations (both horizontal and hierarchical) are involved in collaborative problem solving—as in a community-level planning process or a multi-organization coalition—the concept of fallback is more complex. To understand it, let's look at how formal organizational structures relate to such a process.

**Formal organizations:**
**Power/Authority**
**Decision making**

*Organizations send*
*representatives to the*
*planning process*

**Informal structure:**
**Collaborative**
**Consensus-based**
**Recommending**

**Business**

**Government**

**Community**

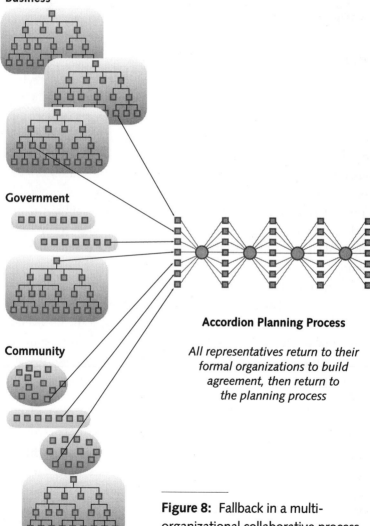

**Accordion Planning Process**

*All representatives return to their*
*formal organizations to build*
*agreement, then return to*
*the planning process*

**Figure 8:** Fallback in a multi-organizational collaborative process

The left side of Figure 8 emphasizes the fact that every community contains a variety of hierarchical and horizontal organizations in its business, government, and community sectors. Just like individual managers, these organizations cannot abdicate their decision-making responsibility and authority to some other formal organization or to a win-lose decision-making vote. But, as the arrows indicate, they can send representatives to participate in an informal, consensus-based, collaborative problem-solving process.

The graphic on the right side of Figure 8 illustrates a multi-organization, collaborative problem-solving process. The larger circles indicate the times when stakeholders (including formal decision makers) from all three sectors convene together under the ground rules of consensus to try to seek agreement phase by phase. The graphic indicates that stakeholder representatives come together and disperse periodically in an attempt to build consensus phase by phase, first in the multi-group collaborative process and then back home in their own organizations. To the extent that consensus can be reached at the end of a collaborative process, stakeholders can return to their positions in their own organizations and act on the agreements. The fallback is that if consensus can't be reached, each stakeholder and his or her organization have the freedom to act independently.

We call this pulsating process of convening and then dispersing an *accordion planning process,* because of the shape of the graphic that diagrams it. It's what allows win-win collaborative processes to coexist with the fallback, win-lose processes of the formal horizontal and hierarchical organizations. The same people participate in both types of structures in parallel. It's the accordion-like movement between these parallel structures that breathes life and power into the process of collaborative action.

To understand one of the benefits of consensus building, the accordion model can be contrasted with the more traditional *linear planning model* in Figure 9. It is often argued that the fewer people you involve in making a decision, the faster you can get your work done. This may be true, but it may then take a long time for you to sell your decision to all the stakeholders who were not included. The real cost of a process in terms of time and resources should be measured from the start of the problem-solving phase to the start of the implementation phase. As Figure 9 illustrates, the problem-solving phase of a linear process may be considerably shorter than a comparable accordion process, which includes all the relevant stakeholders from the beginning. But the selling phase of an accordion process should be much shorter, since all the stakeholders are already on board. You can probably think of a few real-world examples in which linear planning was attempted but the selling time was so lengthy that the project was eventually dropped because of escalating costs or complete deadlock.

## The Benefits of Having a Fallback

The existence of a viable fallback mechanism keeps people engaged in a collaborative process and helps to keep it shorter than it might otherwise be. It may sound counterintuitive, but if you acknowledge that consensus is not always possible, you increase the probability that it will occur. It's often the threat of reverting to the fallback that keeps stakeholders engaged in a consensus-building process. It's the fear of loss of control or the consequences of a win-lose process that keeps everyone engaged. "If we can't reach consensus, the decision will be out of our hands," participants may think. "He (or she, or they) will make the decision for us, and you know what that means...."

I remember facilitating an environmental dispute between ranchers and conservationists in which I said, only partly in jest, "Check your guns at the door, but don't throw them away." The participants could always resort to the weapons of legal action if the collaborative process broke down.

In some conflicts in the public sector, there may be no immediately available, formal venue in which the issue can be resolved, and the fallback may be such lose-lose approaches as a strike, a

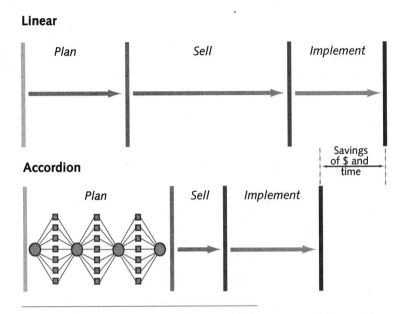

**Figure 9:** Alternative approaches to collaborative problem solving

protest, or outright physical conflict. In many potential disputes, it is the prospect of having to resort to the adversarial, win-lose process of the judicial system or the lose-lose consequences of delay that can re-energize stakeholders and keep them engaged in the process of seeking win-win solutions collaboratively.

Therefore, it's essential before engaging in any collaborative, consensus-based process to clarify both the definition of consensus and the fallback decision-making process. By defining consensus as "everyone buying into the decision," participants will become less anxious that their interests will be ignored or overruled. By clarifying the fallback options, participants understand the consequences of abandoning the process of consensus building.

## Conclusion

To review, the first principle of collaboration asserts that if you can involve all the relevant stakeholders, it is possible to reach consensus most of the time. But the second principle tells us that consensus doesn't just happen. It needs to be built phase by phase. Simply put: If a group can't agree on the problem, it won't be able to agree on the solution. Consensus building can coexist with, and in fact depends on, the fallback decision making of individual managers in a hierarchy, or the majority vote of a board or legislature. Consensus building is an approach to try first, before resorting to win-lose procedures.

When dealing with multiple stakeholders, a collaborative, accordion consensus-building process will take longer than a traditional, top-down, linear approach but, in the end, should progress to the implementation phase more quickly, with significant savings of resources.

These first two principles can't stand alone. Effective collaborative action depends on the skilled application of the remaining three principles—process design, facilitation, and the use of group memory—which we will discuss in subsequent chapters.

# Chapter 4

# Design a Process Map

As you begin to think about participating in or perhaps organizing a collaborative problem-solving process, you will undoubtedly have a host of questions. You might want to know, for example: How long will it take to reach consensus? How will the process work? How much will it cost? What kind of resources will we need? How many committees or task forces will be required? Who will be directly involved and how? How will the rest of the organization or community be included?

Clearly, you'll need answers to these questions before you can move forward. You aren't likely to be satisfied if you are told, "We'll just design the process as we go. We don't know where we are going to end up or even how we are going to get there." While you must remain open about the content of the final decision, you can be more closed and structured about the process of building consensus, as we will see. Organizations and communities can only tolerate so much ambiguity before the work environment becomes counterproductive. Too many degrees of freedom can create confusion and chaos. So, you'll probably want the process to have a visible and understandable structure if you are to feel comfortable about committing to it.

But every context is different. Each involves different stakeholders, different issues, different constraints, different timeframes, and different objectives. And, as we know, problem solving is heuristic: There is no one right way. There is no cookie-cutter process of consensus building that can be applied to all situations.

Moreover, it wouldn't work to try to impose a predesigned process on a group of stakeholders any more than it would to try to sell them on a solution. In fact, it's best if stakeholders buy into and "own" the process by which they reach consensus. Stakeholders need to be able to design, visualize, and manage their own multistakeholder process of collaborative problem solving—in a way that allows flexibility for trial-and-error explorations and does not predetermine the outcome.

Fortunately, it's possible to design in advance a collaborative process—a pathway to reaching consensus—without knowing what that consensus will look like. Thus our third key principle of collaboration is: *Design a process map.* A clear but flexible "road map" will enable you and your fellow stakeholders to navigate with your own content and ultimately arrive at consensus. And all stakeholders can and should be involved in collaboratively designing such a road map.

To understand how process design can work for you, let's explore four elements of this topic:

1. Process design in the context of a *Pathways to Action* model

2. Agenda planning as a kind of simple process design

3. How to read and design process maps

4. How stakeholders can be involved in process design

## Pathways to Action

To grasp the activity of process design, we must use our widest lens—we must pull back a bit and look at the big picture. Figure 10 shows the *spaces* that typically exist in any given collaborative problem-solving process. These spaces are essentially a mental construct for describing the different activities that take place in the course of collaboration. The arrows illustrate the different pathways a group might take to move between the spaces, from process design through implementation.

The left-hand space—process design—involves a kind of problem solving that occurs before the actual content of the issue is tackled. The problems that must be solved here are: How are we going to approach the larger problem? What sequence of steps will we take? Which spaces shall we move through, and in what order? The remaining sections of this chapter cover the process design space in detail.

In the previous chapter, I talked about the problem space and the solution space. As a reminder, in the problem space the task is

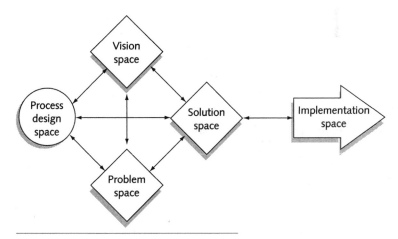

**Figure 10:** The Pathways to Action model

to understand the problem and reach consensus on what it is and why it exists. Problem space, as we saw, can be further divided into three phases: perception, definition, and analysis. In the solution space (with its three phases of alternative generation, evaluation, and decision making), the task is to reach consensus on a solution and a course of action. All collaborative problem solving must end up in the decision-making phase of the solution space before implementation can occur.

As you can see in Figure 10, however, it's not always best to head to the problem space after doing process design. Sometimes it's helpful to jump to the future and work backwards, to explore a *vision* of what your organization or community might look like after the problem is solved. Moving to the vision space takes a group away from the pathology of the immediate problem, builds alignment on a common vision, and generates energy and hopefulness about the future.

Therefore, one of the first tasks of process design is to plan the most promising pathway through these three spaces: problem space, vision space, and solution space. Should we begin in problem space so that everyone has a chance to externalize his or her views of the issue? Or would it be more effective to get away from the specific issue and see if we can get alignment on a vision of where we are headed? Sometimes it makes sense to begin in the problem space to share perceptions of the problem, then jump to the vision space to try to agree on general specifications that solutions to all problems of this type should satisfy, and then return to the problem space to more clearly define and analyze the present problem. As always in human problem solving, there is no one right approach, but one of the tasks in the process design space is to consciously choose the most promising pathway for the given situation.

In the last space—implementation space—stakeholders must implement the solution(s) they agreed to in the solution space. This space completes the heuristic cycle of problem solving. Often, the challenges encountered during implementation generate new issues that need to be addressed, and the whole process of collaborative action begins again in the process design space.

## Agenda Planning as Process Design

To understand what goes on in the process design space, let's first examine the idea of process design as it applies to a single meeting. If you are convening a meeting to try to make a collaborative decision, you won't and can't know in advance exactly what the decision will be. But you can do a great deal of preparation to make sure that the meeting will be effective and to increase the probability that agreements will be reached. This kind of meeting planning is a form of process design. You are thinking in advance about the process of the meeting, not predetermining or manipulating the content of the discussion or the resulting decisions. The product of this kind of process design is the familiar agenda.

Agenda planning is one of the most powerful tools for ensuring the success of a meeting, especially one in which collaborative problem solving will take place. It's amazing how often people go to the effort of inviting people to a meeting and developing a list of substantive items to address, but they don't go further in planning the process of the meeting itself. I have often asked managers what their *desired outcomes* are—what they hope to achieve in a meeting—and have discovered they have only a vague idea.

If you're not clear on the desired outcomes of a meeting, it's hard to design an effective process. Here's where an understanding of the phases of problem solving is useful. Are you trying to agree on a definition of the issue, generate alternatives, or make a final decision? You need to be specific about your desired outcomes, and you need to allow enough time to involve all the stakeholders in the discussion.

At the very least, an effective agenda should contain a clear statement of desired outcomes, identify the relevant stakeholders, clarify the roles that will be played and the decision-making process to be used, and cover the logistics of location, time, and background materials. This information is knowable and should be communicated to participants in advance of the meeting. But it's also possible to plan for the unknowable—to design an agenda for a collaborative problem-solving meeting for which you may only have a vague idea of the problem.

## Developing an Agenda

Let's consider a hypothetical example. Let's say that Pat manages the sales division of a small wholesale company that distributes kitchen and bath hardware to retail stores in the southeastern United States. James, her counterpart in the accounting division, calls to say he is really upset about what he sees as a breakdown in communications between the two divisions. He doesn't have much time to discuss the details at that point, but he insists that two or three people from each division get together to talk about it. James suggests having Maria from human resources serve as facilitator, since he anticipates that the meeting may be contentious. James also says he'll be out of town until just before the meeting, so Pat and Maria should design a tentative agenda.

When Pat meets with Maria to design the agenda, they can go further than cover the basic meeting logistics. Together, they can think their way through a possible flow to the meeting, without knowing much about James's specific concerns. For example, they know that James, and presumably other members of his team, will be coming to the meeting angry. Using the Pathways to Action framework, Pat and Maria know that it may be a good idea to begin in the problem space—specifically, the perception phase of the problem space—offering James and his team an opportunity to present their views and express their emotions. They know that the objective of this phase is "listening and seeking understanding," not "listening and seeking agreement." The purpose will be to acknowledge that there is a legitimate problem that needs to be addressed.

As Maria anticipates how she might handle this segment of the meeting, she may know that one effective process would be to suggest that members of Pat's sales division listen without interruption to what members of the accounting department have to say, and then Pat's side can ask clarifying questions. The idea is to keep the sales team from jumping in too quickly with objections and opposing views. (Such a tactic is called a *facilitative prevention*.) Maria and Pat can estimate it might take five minutes each for James and his two representatives to present their views and answer a few clarifying questions, so perhaps they'll need fifteen minutes in all. The process design for this little segment of the meeting might be expressed in tabular form as follows.

| What<br>(content) | How<br>(process) | Who | Time |
|---|---|---|---|
| "How I see the problem" | Present without interruptions.<br>Questions for clarification only. | James and staff | 15 min.<br><br>15 min. |

The next step in the flow of the meeting might be to have Pat and her representatives present their own views of the communications problem and have the accounting division listen for understanding.

| What<br>(content) | How<br>(process) | Who | Time |
|---|---|---|---|
| "How I see the problem" | Present without interruptions.<br>Questions for clarification only. | Pat and staff | 15 min.<br><br>15 min. |

Then, to bring closure to the perception phase, the facilitator might check for agreement—in other words, check to see that everyone agrees that there is an issue that is important enough to try to resolve together. The group won't be agreeing on a definition of the problem, just that a legitimate and important issue exists, that different people hold different points of view, and that it's time to move on to another phase of problem solving. This step might be expressed as follows.

| What<br>(content) | How<br>(process) | Who | Time |
|---|---|---|---|
| Agreement that there is a problem we need to work on | Discuss/Agree | Maria | 10 min. |

Let's stop for a moment. Pat and Maria have just designed a process for 40 minutes of a meeting knowing very little about the content that will be discussed. It's their knowledge of process (i.e., the spaces, phases, and methods of problem solving) that allows them to do this. Engaging in process design helps to set the meeting up for success by anticipating a sequence of agreement-building phases, deciding what problem-solving methods might be useful in each phase, and estimating how much time it will take to complete each activity. This level of agenda planning can reassure the meeting convenor or senior manager that there is a reasonable strategy for working on the problem. It also prepares the meeting leader with possible tools to handle any conflict that may arise. During the meeting, this level of explicitness about process helps the participants understand what phase of problem solving they are in and what problem-solving methods will be used. After all, in an effectively designed process, all participants should be working on the same problem, in the same phase of problem solving, using the same method.

It's important to keep in mind, however, that an agenda is only a road map from which to consciously deviate. Because there are so many unpredictable dynamics in a group and because problem solving is a heuristic, trial-and-error process, the facilitator will always have to make on-the-spot adjustments and be ready to suggest different problem-solving approaches. But if the facilitator hasn't spent time designing a process, building an agenda, and anticipating tools to use, and only has a limited repertoire of tools, he or she won't be as prepared to make the conscious deviations necessary to keep the process moving forward.

Let's quickly finish the process design for the sample meeting between the sales and accounting departments in order to see what a complete agenda looks like. After getting agreement in the perception phase that there has been a breakdown in communications between the sales and accounting divisions, Maria might suggest jumping to the vision space to explore what ideal working relationships might look like. (Ideally, how would the two divisions be

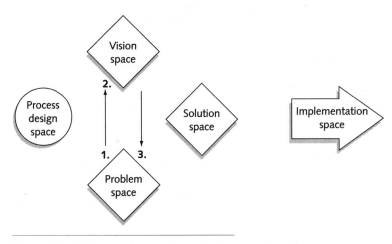

**Figure 11:** Pathway for our hypothetical meeting

treating each other? What information would they be sharing? How often?) Assuming the group reaches some alignment on that vision, it might then return to the problem space to explore more about what the communications breakdown actually was and where and why it happened. That might be enough to accomplish in one meeting.

To review, the meeting would start in the perception phase of problem space, jump to vision space, and return to the analysis and definition phases of problem space, as shown in Figure 11.

If successful, the meeting will allow members of both divisions to listen to and acknowledge each others' perceptions and feelings, establish some alignment on a vision of good relations, and begin to understand what, where, when, and why breakdowns in communications occurred. While not specifically addressing solutions, some obvious ones should fall out of the discussions. Moreover, the meeting itself should open up and reestablish better communications. If the collaborative problem-solving discussions are sandwiched between some normal start-up and closure steps, the written agenda might look something like Figure 12.

| AGENDA | | | |
|---|---|---|---|
| **What**<br>*(content)* | **How**<br>*(process)* | **Who** | **Time** |
| **Start Ups** | | | 8:30–9:00 |
| Welcome | | Pat | 2 min. |
| Introduction of facilitator | | Pat | 1 min. |
| Definition of roles | | Maria | 3 min. |
| Introductions/expectations | | Maria | 10 min. |
| Review/revise agenda | | Maria | 6 min. |
| Ground rules | | Maria | 5 min. |
| Decision making | | Maria | 3 min. |
| **Problem Space—Perception** | | | 9:00–10:10 |
| "How I see the problem" | Present without interruptions. Questions for clarification only. | James and staff | 15 min.<br><br>15 min. |
| | Present without interruptions. Questions for clarification only. | Pat and staff | 15 min.<br><br>15 min. |
| Agreement that there is a problem we need to work on | Discuss/Agree | Maria | 10 min. |
| | *Break* | | *10 mins.* |
| **Vision Space** | | | 10:20–11:10 |
| "What would good working relations look like?" | Individual work Present/clarify | Maria | 10 min.<br>15 min. |
| Common themes | List/discuss | | 15 min. |
| Agreement on vision of good working relationship | List/clarify/build up/ eliminate/check for agreement | | 10 min. |
| **Problem Space–Analysis** | | | 11:10–12:00 |
| What's working about current communications | Brainstorm | Maria | 5 min. |
| What's not working | Brainstorm Clarify/discuss | | 5 min.<br>15 min. |
| Barriers | Brainstorm Clarify/prioritize | | 10 min.<br>15 min. |
| **Next Steps** | | | 12:00–12:30 |
| Outcomes for next meeting | List/discuss/agree | Maria | 10 min. |
| Schedule next meeting | List options/agree | Maria | 10 min. |
| Evaluate meeting | Plus/Delta | Maria | 5 min. |
| Closing statements | Present | Pat/James | 5 min. |

**Figure 12:** A complete agenda for the hypothetical meeting

## Overkill?

This level of process planning may seem like overkill, but I can assure you it's not. It is one of the most powerful facilitative preventions I know—it's a way to anticipate and avoid many of the common meeting problems and barriers to effective collaboration. It forces the meeting convenor and facilitator to think through a meeting step by step, to design an effective pathway to action, to budget time realistically, and to be prepared with alternative strategies so that the facilitator can be "light on her feet" during the meeting. Just going through this planning exercise to create this hypothetical example, I found myself having to make many conscious choices about what problem-solving methods would be appropriate and how much time should be allocated for each activity. It's a good rule of thumb to devote one hour of planning for each hour of actual meeting. Collaborative action does not happen spontaneously. It's important to create the right conditions for success.

It may be unnecessary to present an agenda at this level of detail to all meeting participants, but it's very helpful to have some form of agenda displayed in the meeting room as an aid to both the facilitator and the participants. I've found that one of the simplest and most useful ways to present an agenda is in a "bubble" format. Figure 13 is a bubble agenda for our hypothetical meeting.

The major segments of the meeting are represented as shaded bubbles, with the detailed activities as lines radiating from the bubbles. Connections and flow are indicated by arrows. If the facilitator draws this type of agenda on a sheet of chart pad paper and tapes it to the wall of the meeting room, it will serve as a valuable facilitative aid. This is a simple example of the power of a process map as a facilitative tool. Participants can see at a glance the flow of the meeting and where they are at any point in time. The meeting leader can intervene by pointing to a specific place on the process map to refocus participants on a common process.

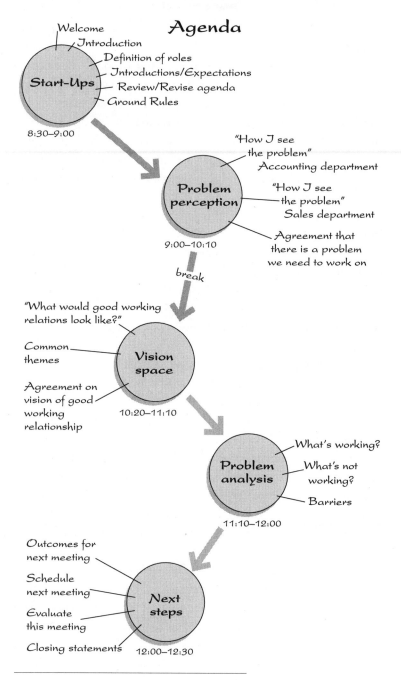

**Figure 13:** Bubble agenda for the hypothetical meeting

## Process Maps

A process map is essentially a complex agenda, typically illustrating a series of meetings over time. It's a tool I've been using for years, and it probably grew out of my architectural training. One of the skills I learned in design school was how to draw and visualize relationships in two- and three-dimensional space. Drawings are simplifications of reality. They can only communicate a limited number of things before they get confusing and unreadable. An architect must be selective about the elements or variables that she wants to present in any one drawing. For example, she may want to examine the circulation pattern of a building (how people will move through a sequence of spaces) or visualize the relative heights of ceilings or the placement of lighting fixtures. Each drawing represents a specific aspect of a design.

As I progressed from thinking about buildings to thinking about problem-solving processes, it was natural for me to apply my graphic skills to process design. I found myself moving from designing buildings to designing collaborative processes where, in a sense, people could become their own architects. The challenge was to figure out what variables to represent.

Since I was trying to visualize a sequence of collaborative activities, I decided that *time* was one variable and *meetings* (and other activities) were the other. As in Figure 14, meetings can be represented by circles (or some other shape), with the sequence and flow of information indicated by connecting lines (with the assumption that time moves forward from left to right on the page). Figure 14 illustrates a simple process in which a large group meets, then breaks into three subgroups, and then reconvenes as a large group.

This kind of diagram, in which shapes represent activities and lines represent connections, is called a *precedence network*. This kind of process map illustrates how and when stakeholders will be involved in collaborative activities, not the activities performed by individuals between meetings.

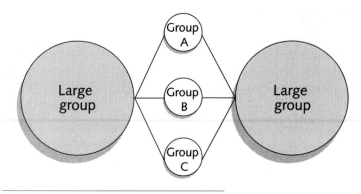

**Figure 14:** A simple process map

### Creating a "Game Board" for Complex Processes

The beauty of process mapping is that you can illustrate even very complex, long-term, multistakeholder collaborative processes in a simple, clear way. Also, process mapping is a means of integrating and implementing stakeholder involvement and consensus building. As you can see in Figure 15, on the horizontal axis you can represent time and, more specifically, block out the phases of the consensus-building process. On the vertical axis, you can represent the rings of involvement discussed in Chapter 2. These two dimensions create a kind of game board on which you can then place specific meetings and other activities.

Figure 15 illustrates a generic organizational planning process. The issue could be anything, from designing a new management structure to deciding how to reduce costs. In this example, eight phases are broken out along the horizontal axis.

1. Education (getting all stakeholders up to speed about the issue)

2. Vision (what it would look like if the problem were solved)

3. Needs (data gathering and fact-finding about the current situation)

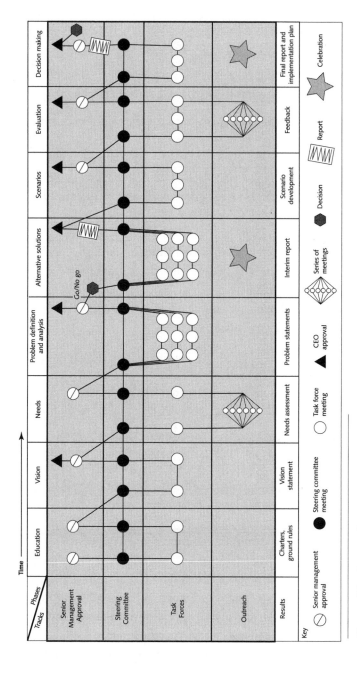

**Figure 15:** A generic process map

4. Problem definition and analysis (breaking the issue into subproblems, defining them, and understanding root causes)

5. Alternative solutions (ways to solve each subproblem)

6. Scenarios (different ways to integrate the solutions to the subproblems)

7. Evaluation (comparing the different scenarios)

8. Decision making (reaching consensus on one integrated solution)

Keep in mind, of course, that each situation or problem will require a unique pathway to action, and, thus, a unique horizontal axis on its process map.

On the vertical axis, our generic example is organized into the following rings of involvement.

1. Senior management approval (with a fallback to the CEO)

2. A steering committee (a group of stakeholders from all divisions of the company who will do most of the work)

3. Task forces (subgroups organized to tackle subproblems and specific scenarios)

4. Outreach (open meetings and other activities to solicit input and react to scenarios as they are developed)

The key at the bottom of the process map explains what the symbols mean.

This level of planning and scheduling is still quite general and abstract. If this process map were applied to a specific project, a real timeline could be plotted along the horizontal axis and dates and times could be assigned to each meeting.

You can easily learn to design these types of process maps.

I have written in more detail about how to construct them in the *Consensus Building Handbook* (Susskind, McKearnan, and Thomas-Larmer, eds., 1999), and courses are offered on the subject by Interaction Associates.

## The Many Benefits of Process Maps

The big idea about process design that's important here is that it's possible to plan a process of collaboration in advance and express it in the form of a graphic process map. The map, as we have seen, can answer such questions as what agreements will be made in what sequence, who will be involved and how, and when specific meetings will be held. These maps can be drawn in greater and greater detail as an effort proceeds, presenting specific dates and times for meetings. The design of these meetings can, in turn, be broken down into detailed agendas. Therefore, it is possible to be quite structured and organized about a process of collaboration that is itself very open in terms of the content of the decisions that will be made.

The process map is a wonderful design tool, much like an architect's drawing for a building. It helps people visualize a process, identify potential problems, and gain a sense of assurance that consensus building will be managed in an organized, methodical manner. In addition, a process map does the following:

- Educates key stakeholders and constituent groups about consensus processes

- Builds support for an effort by demonstrating commitment to thoughtful planning and collaboration

- Illustrates visually how different sets of stakeholders will be included in a process

- Illustrates for key decision makers and resource providers, in a single graphic, the entire flow of a project from start to finish, including the phases, when and how people will be involved, what meetings will be organized, and so forth

- Enables latecomers to quickly understand the flow of a process

- Schedules critical meetings on a common calendar and provides a focal point for resolving complicated issues of sequence and timing

- Reminds individuals of what needs to be done by a certain time

- Orients people toward the broader context and purpose of a meeting or activity

- Facilitates the management of multiple tracks of concurrent activities

- Serves as a working hypothesis from which a group may consciously choose to deviate

- Provides an overview to help a steering committee contemplate the many process issues involved in a collaborative effort

- Acts as a scaffold on which to hang and move new and changing ideas

- Documents what occurs in a project, thereby serving as a historical record

I witnessed the power and value of process maps when my colleagues and I were doing some consulting to Ford Motor Company in the early 1980s. At the time, it was taking Ford and other U.S. car and truck manufacturers at least six years to move from first design concept to the production of a new line of vehicles. The Japanese completed the same product design process in four years. Their secret, it turned out, was to work more collaboratively as a team and involve all the stakeholders, specifically engineering and manufacturing, from the beginning of the product design cycle. This approach has now been widely adopted by most

U.S. manufacturers, but in the '80s Ford was still a very segmented company, organized into separate divisions that essentially "threw" the design "over the walls" from one group to the next. The concept designers would pass the design to the design division, who would pass it on to engineering, who would pass it to manufacturing. Often there were long delays as designs would be passed back to the previous division as unworkable and unacceptable.

At that time, Ford managers used a *timing chart* to graphically present the product development process. This chart depicted the sequence of the planning tasks, but it didn't show how and when the designs were approved at each stage. And since this approval process was the source of the holdups, the chart wasn't very helpful. So, we worked with a committee of stakeholders from all of the divisions in Ford and helped them describe their product development process in terms of the management committees and meetings that were needed to approve a design as it progressed. Using this information, we developed a process map that illustrated the approval process. With this map, the labyrinth of competing bureaucratic committees and lengthy cycles of approval became immediately clear to the committee members. It became obvious that the approval process was an elaborate but classic linear planning approach, in which there were lengthy and costly periods of selling the design from one division to the next.

By mapping out the approval process, the solution became obvious to the committee members. What was needed was more of an accordion approach, one that involved engineering, manufacturing, and even sales from the very beginning of the concept design phase, and one that would build consensus and support phase by phase in the product development cycle. Of course, this proposed approach threatened the turf of the traditional functional divisions in the company, and it took several years for Ford to transition to a team approach to product development. Ultimately, however, Ford was able to cut two years and hundreds of millions of dollars from their product development cycle, and the quality of their cars improved dramatically. The award-winning and best-selling Taurus line was a direct result of this new, collaborative product development process.

## Involving Stakeholders in Process Design

The principle of stakeholder involvement (discussed in Chapter 2) applies to process design, as it does to all kinds of collaborative problem solving. Some consultants simply try to impose the design of a collaborative process on an organization or community, but we think this is a bit hypocritical, and certainly not very helpful in the long run. We believe that stakeholders must own and participate in the design of their collaborative process. Put another way: You must be collaborative about being collaborative.

Take the example of building an agenda for a meeting. In a hierarchical organization, it's a good idea for the convenor or senior decision maker to involve a few participants in designing the agenda for an important meeting. And in a horizontal organization or a multiparty collaboration, it's essential to have a few stakeholders participate in planning a meeting. It's a way of sharing responsibility for the success of the meeting.

At the very least, in the start-up portion of a meeting, there should be an opportunity for all participants to review the proposed agenda, suggest additions and revisions if necessary, and then explicitly agree to follow the agenda. This agreement is a useful tool for the facilitator. Pointing to the agenda posted on the wall, a facilitator might intervene at a difficult moment by saying, "You agreed that we would begin by defining the problem before jumping to solutions. Adam, can you hold on to your idea until we get to the solution space?" If participants agree to an agenda or consciously agree to deviate from it, they will have difficulty claiming afterward that they were controlled or manipulated by the facilitator.

## Organizing a Process Design Committee

The same is true for the design of a more complex, multiparty process. It's best if a *process design committee* (made up of representatives of the key interests) can work collaboratively (with the support of a process consultant, if necessary) to design a collaborative process. The committee can then present this design, in the form of a process map, to the full group of stakeholders for approval. Not only does stakeholder involvement in process design build ownership for the process itself, it also helps educate a subgroup about the principles of collaboration, and it can even demonstrate that consensus is possible.

One of my most memorable experiences with a process design committee occurred during the Newark Collaboration Group, the public-private partnership I discussed in Chapter 2. At the outset of this process, about sixty business, nonprofit, and government leaders, including the mayor of Newark, attended a community meeting. They discussed the many critical problems facing the city, noted that the adversarial relationships among community leaders was hindering attempts to resolve the problems, and agreed, at a minimum, to explore how a more collaborative, consensus-based planning process might help. They selected a process design committee from among the stakeholders present. The process design committee agreed to meet several times and return to the large group with a proposal for a consensus-building process.

Because the level of trust between the sectors was so low, we ended up with thirty people on the process design committee. Even then, many participants had trouble focusing on process design until they were convinced that the other stakeholder groups were sincere about committing resources and working collaboratively. After many heated exchanges and hard work, the committee agreed on three short-term projects that would demonstrate the willingness of all sectors to commit resources to the city and work collaboratively. These projects included a summer employment program for youth, progress on a moderate-income housing project that had stalled, and the cleanup of a main street that connected the city to the airport. The projects were presented to the group of sixty for their approval, and then undertaken immediately. The fact that the process design committee participants could negotiate with each other, make agreements by consensus, and produce results fueled their belief in the power of collaborative action. Often, these types of spin-off projects are necessary to address immediate issues, demonstrate the collective capacity to get things done, and keep stakeholders energized and engaged during the problem-solving phase.

The process map for the Newark Collaboration Group is shown in Figure 16. The map reveals that after the first large-group meeting in May, the process design committee met twice and returned to the June meeting with their proposed short-term projects. Immediately afterward, a track of activity called "Specific Programs" was initiated to include these projects.

Once the members of the Newark process design committee had demonstrated to each other that they could reach consensus and commit resources for some short-term projects, they were ready to turn to the task of process design with great interest and enthusiasm. They reviewed and revised some basic principles of collaboration (similar to what I've been presenting so far), researched and visited a number of other public-private partnerships, agreed on a set of phases and rings of involvement, and produced the process map in Figure 16.

The presentation they gave to the large group in July was one of the most persuasive and well-thought-out arguments for the power of collaborative action that I have ever heard. The members of the process design committee were great advocates for the process they had designed, and the proposal was quickly approved and funded. It was their process and they owned it. Many members of the process design committee volunteered to serve on the steering committee for the next phase, ensuring a continuity of

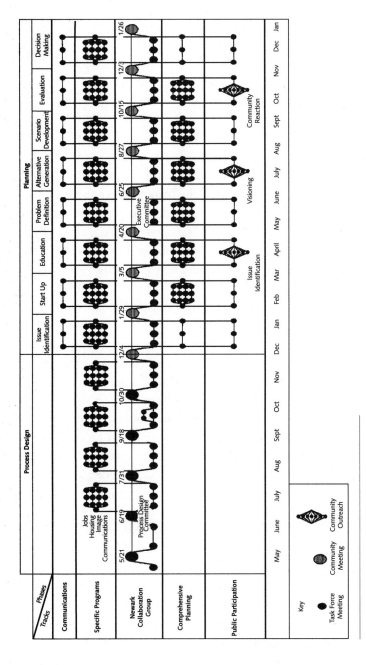

**Figure 16:** Process map for the Newark Collaboration Group

experience and process knowledge in the group that was to guide the effort over the next year. The steering committee continued to revise the process map to reflect which meetings had actually been held and when meetings were scheduled, and they used the map to orient participants in each of the large-group sessions.

## Conclusion

The five principles in this part of the book form a constellation of ideas about collaborative action. Each idea is powerful in and of itself and speaks to both our hearts and minds. Taken together, these actionable principles offer a hopeful and actionable view of the world. Let's review the first three and how they work together.

The idea of stakeholder involvement is that it is possible and necessary to involve from the beginning of a collaborative planning process representatives of all the stakeholder groups (including those affected by the decision as well as those with the authority to make decisions), and that the power of collaborative action comes from inclusion, not exclusion. The idea of consensus building is that it is possible to reach consensus (with everyone able to agree to and support a decision) most of the time, but agreements must be built phase by phase, and conscious choices must be made about which pathway to take. In general, you must agree on the problem before jumping to solutions, and a fallback decision-making process should be clarified from the beginning in the event that consensus can not be reached. The idea behind process design is that it's possible to plan a structured but flexible process of collaboration without knowing or predetermining the content of the decisions that will be made. These process designs will have an accordion (rather than linear) pattern to them and can be expressed as process maps that offer a kind of game board for visualizing, modifying, and managing a multitrack process of collaboration.

The promise underlying these ideas is that it's possible to build consensus among all stakeholders through a structured process of collaborative action. The message of these ideas is that you must build consensus phase by phase and provide multiple ways for stakeholders to be involved. Once we accept the possibility and practicality of collaboration, as well as its underlying values and benefits, we can't help but be called to action. It just doesn't make sense not to collaborate. The next two ideas—facilitation and group memory—ensure that when we try to collaborate face-to-face in meetings, the experience is positive and productive.

Chapter 5

# Designate a Process Facilitator

Most collaborative processes involve face-to-face meetings, and the effectiveness of those meetings is critical to the success of the collaborative effort. The effectiveness of any single meeting is largely dependent on how well *process* issues are handled—issues such as developing an agenda, deciding which heuristic problem-solving strategy to use when, ensuring that everyone has a chance to speak, handling conflicts among participants, and so forth. The best way to deal with these process issues is through the use of a dedicated, neutral process guide called a *facilitator*.

Facilitated meetings today are being conducted around the world, in the public and private sectors, and in every conceivable situation and context. You've undoubtedly taken part in meetings run by a facilitator. Indeed, the concept has become very popular. But along with the widespread acceptance of facilitation has come, in places, an associated misunderstanding, trivialization, and even abuse of the practice. Perhaps you've had bad experiences with facilitators who do nothing more than call on people to speak, or who are clearly not impartial or neutral, or who use their position to manipulate the discussion. Perhaps you've even felt that the facilitator hindered problem solving, rather than facilitating it. Unfortunately, lots of people who are called upon to facilitate have no idea how the concept evolved or what functions they should serve in a meeting. This chapter will shed some light on these topics.

It's essential, after all, that facilitation be done right. What happens in meetings—people's attitudes, behaviors, mindsets, and so forth—is a microcosm of what will happen in a larger, long-term collaborative project or in an organization or community that's trying to work more collaboratively. So facilitation, or process expertise, is in fact important to every level of collaboration—from small groups to entire communities. Also, a facilitator may have a multitude of responsibilities outside of meetings, involving planning, keeping stakeholders engaged in a process, and so forth. Because facilitation is so central to collaboration, it's essential that the rationale for the role and functions of the facilitator be clearly understood.

This chapter isn't a how-to guide to facilitation. Many organizations (my company among them) offer training in facilitation skills, and many books offer helpful instruction, as well. My former partner, Michael Doyle, and I described the *Interaction Method* of facilitating meetings in detail in our book *How to Make Meetings Work* (1976). An updated and abridged discussion of the topic can be found in Chapter 7 of *The Consensus Building Handbook* (Susskind, McKearnan, and Thomas-Larmer, eds., 1999). These and other books deal with the tools and techniques involved in facilitation.

This chapter, by contrast, will focus on the ideas underlying facilitation. I'll look at the roots of the concept, discuss the system of four self-correcting roles in meetings, and describe the four key functions of the facilitator. Each of the functions addresses a set of challenges to effective collaboration, and leads toward the promise of a more productive and humane work environment. In the course of the chapter, I will also talk about the impact facilitation has had on my company, our clients, and me. My hope is that if you fully grasp the ideas underlying facilitation—if you truly have them in your heart, to use the words of the Eastern Europeans mentioned in the Introduction—then you, too, will be able to "sing."

## The Roots of Facilitation

Facilitated, task-oriented problem solving evolved during the 1960s and '70s as a response to many societal forces. I'm not sure that anyone can claim to have "invented" it. While my colleagues at Interaction Associates and I certainly played a significant role in formalizing the idea of facilitation into the Interaction Method, and in training hundreds of thousands of people over the years, we freely acknowledge that we adopted and assimilated ideas promoted by other individuals and organizations.

The word *facilitator* was being used in the '60s to refer to the leaders of sensitivity training and encounter groups. The focus of these activities was personal growth, not group problem solving, and the role of the facilitator was more like that of a therapist in a group session. However, the word was gaining currency as a label for someone who oversaw process issues for a group, so Michael Doyle and I chose to retain and redefine it in the context of a more active, task-oriented role within the Interaction Method of running meetings.

The '60s was a natural time for the concept of facilitation to emerge. I first glimpsed the potential of facilitation in creative problem solving while attending a training session in 1965 run by an organization called Synectics. (I'll talk about that experience a bit later in the chapter.) When I moved to Berkeley, California, in 1968, I found a perfect testing ground for my emerging ideas about process and group problem solving.

These were exciting times for those of us coming of age, and Berkeley was one of the national hot spots for the evolution of new ideas. Student activism, war protests, the women's movement, the rise of Black Power, communal living, and the exploration of new freedoms were taking place in many areas. Young people were driven to break out of old norms and develop viable alternatives and new approaches to almost everything: education, housing, music, dress, even sex. In addition, there was a demand for new forms of alternative dispute resolution and citizen participation— for ways to enable people to become more directly involved in the development of their own communities. In businesses, there was a need to engage teams of front-line workers in improving the quality of their products and services. Looking back on it now, I see that the idea of facilitation was a natural response to many of these forces.

Facilitation was also the answer to my personal quest to find my path in life. My colleagues and I were full of youthful energy to change the world. We wanted to have a meaningful impact on all sorts of social issues that went way beyond the scope of any content-based profession like architecture. We did not want to be restricted to any one field, issue, or geography. Our mission was to help people become "the architects of their own futures" by giving them tools, not solutions. Our vision was to work on the world's most significant issues, with the brightest and most knowledgeable people, in the most supportive environments, using the best available technology. These were lofty goals. But we realized that we could achieve them if we worked as facilitators. Facilitation was a perfect means of accessing important groups of people working on critical issues.

## Shared Responsibility and the Interaction Method

To understand the concept of facilitation, let's look first at how it fits into the Interaction Method that Michael Doyle and I developed. The Interaction Method for managing meetings was built around the idea of shared responsibility—the idea that responsibility for the success of a meeting should be shared among all participants, and that the necessary functions and roles should be differentiated and not all put in the hands of a single person. After all, effective collaboration in a meeting involves handling many different challenges, such as traffic problems (making sure everyone has a chance to speak), process battles (deciding how to proceed, what problem-solving strategy to use), record keeping (capturing what has been said to avoid repetition and wheel spinning), setting constraints (choosing which issues are to be discussed and which aren't), and decision making (determining what happens if consensus can't be reached). It's difficult, if not impossible, for one person to pay attention to all of these things at once. Yet all these issues have to be handled. The idea of shared responsibility offers a way out of this dilemma by differentiating roles— asking different people to attend to different aspects of a meeting.

The four roles and functions in the Interaction Method are: facilitator, recorder, leader, and group member. (See Fig. 17 on page 112.) The facilitator, as we'll discuss in this chapter, focuses on process. The recorder writes group members' ideas on chart pad paper in front of the room, for all to see. (We'll talk about this role in detail in the next chapter.) The leader is the senior manager in the meeting. Usually, this is the person who will make the decision if consensus can't be reached in the meeting. The leader helps to make sure that the group stays focused on the right content and task, but he or she does not run the meeting. Finally, the group members focus on the actual problem solving.

The Interaction Method is *self-correcting* in that everyone in a meeting shares responsibility for making sure that everyone else stays *in role*, thereby ensuring that individuals don't overstep their function or manipulate the group.

### The Interaction Method, in Practice

Let's look at how the Interaction Method works in practice, using a hypothetical example.

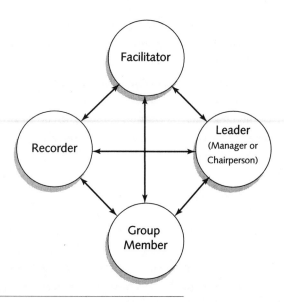

**Figure 17:** The four self-correcting roles of the Interaction Method *(For a more complete presentation of the Interaction Method, please refer to the Resources section.)*

Let's say that ten people from the ACME Manufacturing Company are settling into their conference room for a meeting. Eight chairs have been configured in a semicircle facing a wall, on which sheets of chart pad paper have been taped in four neat stacks, five deep. Akiko, the CFO (and meeting leader, in this case) and seven members of her accounting staff are taking their seats. Luis, the facilitator, and Justin, the recorder, sit facing the group on either side of the chart paper.

"Good morning," Akiko begins. "I've called this meeting because we're facing a problem that must be resolved quickly. The average time it takes us to collect accounts receivables after we've sent an invoice has slipped from sixty-one to eighty-three days. This is causing a significant cash crunch for ACME. Senior management is upset, and I promised we'd take immediate action to get us back to our goal of sixty days."

Akiko continued: "We need to understand the root causes of this problem and figure out what we can do to correct it. I'm too angry and involved to run this meeting impartially, so I've asked Luis from human resources to facilitate and Justin from information services to record. They'll explain their roles and help us build an agenda. We'll go for consensus, but the fallback is to me. That is, if we can't reach consensus here I'll have to make a decision myself. I don't want to leave this room until we get a handle on what's going on and what we're going to do to fix it."

At this point, Luis, the facilitator, stands up and begins to speak. "Good morning," he says. "I know many of you have participated in facilitated meetings before, but I would still like to review my role and ask for your support. As facilitator, my role is to be neutral and nonevaluative. I'm not going to contribute my ideas or evaluate yours. I may offer process suggestions, but my role is to stay out of the content of the meeting and make sure everyone has a chance to be heard. This is your meeting, and I'm here to serve you. Please help me to stay in my role as facilitator. If any of you feels that I'm not being neutral or that I'm leading you in a direction you don't want to go, please let me know and I'll do whatever I can to correct the situation. Any questions?"

Everyone shakes his or her head "no." "OK, then. Justin, will you review your role?"

Justin then explains his purpose at the meeting. "I'm here as your recorder," he says. "My role is to capture your comments and ideas on these sheets of paper in your own words. I may edit, but I will try not to paraphrase. Please let me know if I miss something important, if I don't record your idea accurately, or if you can't read my handwriting. And I apologize in advance for any misspellings— I'm a lousy speller. So let me know if I mess up. Any questions?"

There are no questions, so Luis, the facilitator, takes over once again. "Let's get started," he says. "Akiko, would you clarify what you see as the desired outcomes of this meeting?"

"Sure," Akiko responds, as Justin stands poised to write on the chart pad paper. "I would hope that by the end of this meeting we will all understand and agree on why we have slipped twenty-three days in the collection of our receivables. Second, I hope we can agree on a set of immediate actions we can take to correct the situation—including a clear idea of who is going to do what, by when."

Akiko glances up at what Justin is writing and realizes he's made a mistake. "No, Justin, I said 'twenty-three' days, not 'twenty.'"

"Oops! Sorry," Justin replies. "Thanks for correcting me."

"Any questions about these outcomes?" Luis asks. "Are there any you can't agree to?"

Lisa, the controller, pipes up. "Akiko, I agree we need to understand why we have slipped so badly in the last few months. And we certainly need to agree on what actions we can take. But do you think it's reasonable to finalize deadlines during this meeting? We may need to get some more information, especially from our IT department, before we can commit to specific dates."

"You may be right, depending on the fix," Akiko says. "Let's go for agreement in this meeting on the basic solutions and finalize the work plans tomorrow."

Luis takes the reigns again. "So, with that adjustment to the desired outcomes, are we ready to move on?"

"Wait a sec. I had my hand up." It's George, the data specialist. "I don't agree that we have definitely slipped a full twenty-three days across the board. I think we need to do some more analysis."

"Well, we're not trying to agree on an exact definition of the problem just yet," Luis says, "only some desired outcomes for the meeting. What phrasing would work for you?

"Let's just say '...agree on why we have slipped *so much*' instead of giving a number of days," George suggests. "Then we can try to be more specific once we have done some more analysis."

"Is that acceptable to you, Akiko?" Luis asks.

"Sure, I can live with that for now."

"Justin, will you make that change, please?" Luis asks. "Thanks.

Any more changes to the desired outcomes? OK? Everybody ready to move on?"

With that, their substantive discussion of the problem begins.

In this short example, you can see how the self-correcting mechanism of the Interaction Method works through a set of *social contracts*. The facilitator, for example, explicitly asked for help from participants, requesting and empowering group members to push back if they feel he is not staying in role or is leading them in a direction they don't want to go. When participants in a facilitated meeting agree to speak out if the facilitator steps out of role, they are assuming a measure of responsibility for the success of the meeting. Likewise, the facilitator keeps the leader from dominating the meeting, while the leader and group members ensure that the facilitator and recorder stay neutral and in role. Through the Interaction Method, then, the traditional architecture of meetings is fundamentally altered from one person controlling both process and content to a set of differentiated, self-correcting roles and shared responsibilities. Like a gyroscope in the auto-pilot guidance system of an airplane, the system can correct itself and get back on track. Power and responsibility are distributed in order to avoid abuse and to ensure that all the important aspects of meetings are covered.

It may seem counterintuitive, but the fact is that when the roles in small-group problem solving are explicit and differentiated, collaboration is likely to be more effective. When roles get blurred, when it's not clear who is attending to process, collaboration may fall apart. For example, most novice facilitators feel nervous at the opening of a meeting and tend to rush through the contracting phase. It may feel uncomfortable to make these social contracts explicit, but facilitators who skip over them effectively disable the self-correcting mechanism. The facilitator can't just say, "I'm going to be your facilitator today. Any questions?" He or she must share responsibility by asking participants to help keep in role. "Please let me know if you feel I'm not being neutral or leading you in a direction you don't want to go. This is your meeting, not mine.

You must help to make it work. Will you help me? Do you agree?" It is through this explicit agreement that the facilitator places a significant part of the responsibility for the success of the meeting into the hands of the group members.

### Results, Process, and Relationships

There's another benefit to sharing responsibility that has to do with measuring the success of a collaborative process. We feel strongly that the *results* of a meeting (e.g., whether agreement was reached or not) represent only one dimension of success. The other important dimensions are *process* and *relationships*. (See fig. 18.) For a collaborative effort to be considered successful, participants must be satisfied with all three dimensions. For example, if you are a meeting participant and you don't like the process used to arrive at an agreement, or if you don't feel like your concerns were adequately heard, you will not be very satisfied with the effort. That's true even if you feel OK about the final agreement. The same is true if, say, you don't like how others behaved at the meeting, or if you ended up feeling hurt, angry, resentful, or more distant from another group member. Again, you won't be satisfied in these situations even if the group achieved a good substantive result.

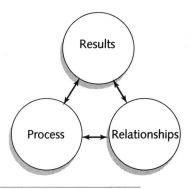

**Figure 18:** The three dimensions of success

The Interaction Method ensures that all three dimensions of success will be adequately handled, because the four roles in the Method are each responsible for one or more dimensions. The facilitator and recorder focus primarily on process and relationships. The leader and the group members are thus freed to focus on the results, or content, of the meeting. Thus, the shared responsibility created by the Interaction Method helps to ensure that success is achieved on all three dimensions: results, process, and relationships.

## The Four Functions of the Facilitator

Let's look now at the four functions of a facilitator. I alluded to them in the hypothetical example above, but I want to address each one in some detail here, since these concepts are so fundamental to collaboration and so often misunderstood. The four functions are

- the facilitator as process guide;

- the facilitator as tool giver;

- the facilitator as neutral third-party; and

- the facilitator as process educator.

### The Facilitator as Process Guide

In any conversation there is *process* (how people are interacting) and *content* (what they are talking about). It's very difficult, as mentioned above, for one person to handle both process and content aspects of a discussion simultaneously. It's just too complicated, and it often leads to unproductive meetings. It also allows one person—the person running the meeting—to easily manipulate the discussion to his or her own ends. For example, managers, leaders, and committee chairs who run their own meetings may be inclined (sometimes unconsciously) to promote their own ideas and to ignore, put off, or criticize group members with whom they disagree.

A fundamental point of facilitation, then, is to separate process leadership from content leadership—to place the guidance of the process of collaboration in the hands of someone who agrees to be neutral and serve at the will of the group. The manager or chair still retains content leadership and final decision-making authority, but is freed to focus on the issues rather than on leading the discussion. This also frees the group from potential manipulation problems.

A facilitator, therefore, is a *process guide*; he or she does not evaluate or contribute substantive ideas to a discussion. The facilitator is the servant of the group, not its leader, and works to ensure that the group accomplishes its goals. He or she does this by offering process suggestions, enforcing ground rules agreed to by the group, keeping discussions on track, protecting group members from attack, and ensuring that all members participate.

The facilitator's control comes from helping group members to make process agreements (e.g., "First we'll brainstorm ideas, then evaluate them. Any objections to that?") and then holding participants to those commitments. Facilitation is the art of making and building upon many small agreements about process and content. The facilitator is also typically responsible for the logistical arrangements for meetings and for developing an agenda (with the leader and the input of group members) before a meeting.

The implication of this concept is simple: *If you are a leader, manager, or a chair of a group or organization, you should seriously consider not running your own meetings.* You should instead ask someone within your organization who does not have a stake in the issues to facilitate, or you should hire an outside facilitator. And I don't just mean for important meetings—I mean for most of your meetings. It really is possible to delegate the facilitator role, even in hierarchical organizations and groups that operate by *Robert's Rules of Order.* Many managers and leaders who profess to foster collaboration simply dismiss this idea as impossible or unnecessary, but others have discovered that it's fundamental to the concept of collaboration.

I believe it's a conflict of interest for a leader to run a meeting when he or she has a large stake in the subject matter. To do so is akin to one person trying to be player, captain, coach, and referee all at the same time.

Years ago, when we were first trying to convince senior managers that it would be to their advantage to let someone else facilitate their meetings, we used another helpful analogy. We asked them: "If you were having a meeting with your associates in a car on the way to the airport, would you want to be driving the car, as well? It's a waste of your time and energy. Let someone else drive. Let someone else be your meeting chauffeur."

As leaders and their teams become more aware of process and more skilled at using facilitative behaviors, it may become possible for one person to play more than one role. For example, a leader may also facilitate, or one person may facilitate, record, and even participate. In these cases, it is important that each person be clear about which role they are playing at each point in time. And in large-group or high-conflict situations, it really is essential to differentiate the four roles of the Interaction Method.

I first experienced the power of facilitation as a *client* in 1970. At the time, I was playing way too many roles in our little mission-driven organization: founder, investor, expert, and leader. There was no way I could be neutral and unbiased about some of the growth issues we were facing. I remember a decision we faced when we finished the work funded by our first Carnegie Foundation grant. We had demonstrated that students in the sixth and ninth grades could learn and apply new problem-solving heuristics, and we needed to decide what the next logical step was in our effort to show that problem-solving skills could be taught in schools. It appeared we needed to demonstrate that teachers could learn to teach process in the context of their normal subjects. But working with teachers and dealing with the bureaucracy of school districts would require expertise, experience, and motivation that few, if any, of us had. The questions were: Who in our organization was willing to sign up for this next step? And what would happen to those who were not interested in or capable of designing and conducting teacher training?

These were difficult questions, and the answers had the potential to drive us apart. I couldn't facilitate the pivotal meeting at which this would be discussed. I was clearly too involved, and I wanted to be able to focus on the content of the discussions, rather than on the process. So we asked Geoff Ball, an early independent facilitator (who is still working in the field), to facilitate. The four of us who comprised Interaction Associates at the time took part—Chris and Ruth Thorsen, who had run the school programs with me, Ethan Glück, a classmate of mine from design school who had joined our team, and me. We met in the basement of my house in the Berkeley Hills, which we had converted into an office and a meeting room specifically designed to support facilitated problem solving. One wall was illuminated by track lighting and had a special surface on which sheets of newsprint could be mounted using masking tape or push pins. The floor was carpeted, and we sat in a semicircle on comfortable chairs facing Geoff, who both facilitated and recorded ideas on the newsprint.

I remember so vividly how relieved and liberated I felt to have someone else serve as facilitator—to have someone else worry about staying neutral and making sure that everyone had a chance to participate. I could still participate actively as leader and participant, but I didn't have to worry about the process. I could focus on what was best for my organization and my friends. Just the act of delegating control of the process to him avoided the potential that I or anyone else would manipulate and discredit the meeting. The meeting was memorable both because of its strategic importance and because it was a demonstration of the power of collaborative action. All the powerful ideas about collaboration were at work here: stakeholder involvement, consensus building, the use of group memory, facilitative leadership—all of them.

The group engaged in difficult conversations, but Geoff's skilled facilitation prevented the meeting from blowing apart. He freed us all to define and deal separately with two sets of issues: first, what would be best for Interaction Associates, and, second, what would be best for us as individuals. In the end, we agreed that what was logical and necessary for our enterprise was different from what each of us wanted or were skilled to do. I agreed to recruit someone new to lead the teacher-training effort. Ethan agreed to focus his energies on developing a service to facilitate the interactions of architects with their clients (an idea we'd been toying with for some time). And Chris and Ruth decided they would return to the their previous practice of conducting experiential workshops for students. Essentially, we split up, with Ethan and me remaining at Interaction Associates and Chris and Ruth leaving. But we had come to this decision very harmoniously. Although we were sad we wouldn't be working closely together any more, we all fully supported the decision, felt it was right, felt good about the process, and were able to maintain our friendships. We wouldn't have gotten there without Geoff's facilitation.

### The Facilitator as Tool Giver

Collaborative problem solving depends on the selection and focused application of appropriate problem-solving processes in meetings. For collaboration to succeed, all group members need to be working on the same substantive content using the same process, at the same time. Otherwise, you get what we call the *multiheaded animal syndrome*—everyone heading off in a different direction using a different process. So, another function of the facilitator is to be a *tool giver*. A facilitator should be skilled in a broad repertoire of problem-solving and decision-making methods. It's the facilitator's job to offer process suggestions and to make sure the group is clear, at any given time, about which method it's using, and why.

I had my first glimpse of the power of tool giving when, as a graduate student in 1965, I went to a training session run by Synectics, Inc., a consulting firm that specialized in fostering creativity and innovation in groups. George Prince and Bill Gordon, the founders of Synectics, developed a creative problem-solving methodology that involved breaking fixation by leading a group on a metaphorical journey away from the problem at hand, looking for analogies in unrelated fields, and then force-fitting the new ideas back onto the original problem. This heuristic problem-solving method often led to new insights and breakthroughs.

The session took place in a cozy meeting room in Synectics' Harvard Square office in Cambridge, Massachusetts. The participants sat in overstuffed sofas and chairs facing a wall on which pads of chart paper had been hung from hooks. The meeting leader led the group through the Synectics process, calling on participants, asking questions, and suggesting specific problem-solving methods. (For instance, he asked participants to share what they liked about an idea before offering criticisms of it.) He also recorded the ideas on the paper.

Although I was purportedly studying architecture at the time, I had become increasingly interested in the nature of problem solving—in how humans solved problems both individually and in groups. I quickly recognized that the Synectics sessions contained all the elements of a new and effective approach to running meetings. I had had my first look at the power of having a neutral facilitator run a collaborative problem-solving session.

I don't think Prince or Gordon realized at that time that the structure of their Synectics sessions—particularly the use of the leader as process tool giver—could be generalized to almost any kind of meeting or collaborative problem-solving situation. Nonetheless, I owe these two men a great debt of gratitude for offering me a glimpse of the future. The ideas sparked by that meeting have been altered and refined by my colleagues and me at Interaction Associates over the past three decades and have become the basis of much of our work.

## The Facilitator as Neutral Third-Party

The next important function of the facilitator is to serve as a neutral and unbiased *third party*. The Newark Collaboration Group, which I've discussed in previous chapters, provides a good example of how this function works. The Newark project, as you will recall, was initiated by Prudential Financial, which wanted to help revitalize the city rather than simply move its headquarters elsewhere. Alex Plinio, then vice president for public affairs at Prudential, was the initiator and first champion of the project. It was his idea to organize the inaugural meeting of sixty leaders from the business, government, and nonprofit sectors to discuss the city's problems.

As Alex thought about how to organize the meeting, he quickly realized that he should not be the one to run it. He could play an important leadership role, but if he tried to run the meeting it might be seen (by representatives of the government and nonprofit sectors) as an attempt by the private sector to control the agenda. He knew, and he believed others knew, that the person who controls the process of a meeting can assert undue influence on the outcome of the meeting. If the meeting had any chance of success, the leadership of the process had to be placed in the hands of someone who was both skilled in group problem-solving processes and perceived as impartial.

So, Alex asked me to serve as an unbiased, neutral facilitator. Alex was clearly demonstrating that he was willing to relinquish control and trust the process.

The meeting itself was a classic demonstration of the power of facilitation and shared responsibility. Since few of the participants had experienced facilitation before, I spent a significant amount of time defining the role and establishing my contract with the group. "This is your meeting, not mine," I said. "I'm here as your servant. Let me know if at any point you feel I'm not being neutral or am manipulating you in any way." I reviewed the agenda, asked for additions or revisions, and then checked for agreement. Then I did the same for a list of suggested ground rules.

There were a few early tests of my neutrality, as there almost always is when the level of distrust in a group is so high. "My hand was up first." "That's not exactly what I said." "Wait a moment. I've got something else to add." By not responding defensively, by acknowledging my unintentional "mistakes," I was able to win the trust of the group. The meeting was a great success. The group of Newark leaders reached consensus that a process design committee should be formed to return within a month with a plan for how to proceed collaboratively.

As in the Newark case, there are times when no one in an organization or community is perceived as unbiased enough to be trusted to conduct a fair and inclusive meeting. But an outside facilitator can step in and serve as a neutral third party in these situations.

We have an exercise in our advanced facilitation courses called "Get the Facilitator," in which a small group tries to stop the facilitator from facilitating by challenging his or her neutrality, legitimacy, credibility, or experience. Even in this extreme situation, a condition one would rarely experience in real life, a skilled facilitator can facilitate while demonstrating non-defensiveness and a willingness to serve the group. Facilitation is similar to the martial arts, in that the facilitator takes the energy of the group (however negative) and guides it in a constructive direction. When a facilitator's neutrality is questioned, he or she might say, "You're concerned that I'm going to favor management's point of view. That's a legitimate concern. Will you watch me like a hawk and let me know if I do anything that seems like I'm being biased in my facilitation? Are you willing to work for an hour and see if we get anywhere?" Little by little, the facilitator can take the concerns of the group, legitimize them, sequence them, and make small agreements that begin to turn the energy of the group from attacking the facilitator to working constructively on the problem.

Facilitated, multiparty collaborative problem solving has become an accepted and widely used approach to resolving public-sector conflicts from the community level to the national level. Stakeholder groups from all sectors have learned the value of having potentially explosive meetings conducted by an experienced, third-party facilitator. Likewise, organizations are increasingly using outside facilitators to run important, high-conflict meetings. They understand that the facilitator's function of neutrality, along with his or her role of providing process guidance, tool giving, and process education, adds great value to their meetings.

## The Facilitator as Process Educator

Since 1969, our mission at Interaction Associates has been "... to demonstrate the power and *transfer the skills* of collaborative action." This mission, I believe, should apply to all who serve as facilitators. Facilitators must be willing to educate participants about process as they facilitate.

Many people have never experienced the power of facilitation, and group members can get discouraged about the possibility of working constructively together. The facilitator knows, however (or ought to know!), that consensus is possible—that, most of the time, if the concepts described in this book are applied effectively, collaboration does work. The facilitator's job, then, is to demonstrate that by applying a few simple concepts—such as good process planning, role clarification, and the use of basic problem-solving tools—productive collaboration is not only possible, it is probable.

To act responsibly, facilitators must dismount from their white horses and demystify what they are doing. They should transfer the tools of collaborative action as they work so that group members learn facilitative behaviors. While formal training in teamwork and facilitation skills is recommended for everyone as an efficient way to build capacity within a group or organization, a good facilitator can significantly raise the level of process awareness and process education in a group while facilitating.

There are many techniques that allow him or her to do so, but the underlying strategy is that of externalizing facilitative and problem-solving processes. A facilitator can do this with a very light but effective touch. A few words about why he or she is doing something can be enough. For example, a facilitator can acknowledge when the group has reached a strategic moment: "OK, we have just finished brainstorming a list of ideas. We are at a strategic moment. We have several choices as to how to proceed. There are several ways we could organize and order this list. One of them might be to review the list and clarify those that you don't understand. Or we could begin by eliminating those that are obvious duplicates. I would recommend that you begin by clarifying first so that you are certain you understand what was intended by each item before you merge or combine it with another. Any objections?" Facilitators can also offer little educational "commercials" such as, "Remember, problem solving is heuristic. There is no one right way. Let's try one approach, see if it works, and, if not, we'll try another." Such comments can greatly help to avoid process battles.

Facilitators should not limit the educating of participants to teaching skills or tools. They should also communicate the *mindsets* and *heart-sets* behind facilitation—the attitudes, values, and beliefs underlying the practice. Each of the principles of collaboration in this book is rooted in values and beliefs about what people are capable of doing together. Some that I've already discussed include the belief that human problem solving is heuristic, and that problem-solving skills can be learned and taught. Also, collaboration itself rests on the fundamental values of respect for human dignity and the right of stakeholder involvement. The practice of facilitation is and should be concerned with the promotion of these beliefs and values, which themselves lie at the heart of our democracy.

A skilled facilitator can, by modeling effective facilitative attitudes, tools, and behaviors over the course of a series of meetings, move a group a long way toward becoming more educated about group problem-solving processes. Ultimately, and particularly with small groups, the facilitator may actually educate himself or herself out of a job. The more process aware and educated a group or team becomes, the more the function of facilitator can be passed around, the more everyone can contribute facilitative process suggestions, and the more the group can become self-correcting and self-facilitating. At some point, an external facilitator may no longer be needed.

## Conclusion

Facilitation is one of those ideas that simply works. As an approach to running meetings, it has been applied in almost every conceivable situation around the world. I have facilitated meetings for grassroots community organizations, corporate boards, congressional retreats, and international conferences. The role of facilitator is effective in all of these diverse settings, and it seems acceptable and adaptable to most cultures. It has been a great personal joy to see the idea of facilitation spread so widely.

To sum up, facilitation, as an approach to leading collaborative meetings, works because it:

- promotes and supports consensus building and the search for win-win solutions;

- can be used in conjunction with any problem-solving method or planning process;

- shares responsibility with participants and encourages them to be more facilitative themselves—in other words, it builds in a set of checks and balances among meeting participants;

- helps participants make conscious choices about content and process—what they want to talk about and how they want to do it;

- prevents the individual with the most positional power or the most content expertise from controlling a meeting;

- ensures that everyone has a chance to participate in a meeting;

- ensures that everyone in a meeting will work on the same problem using the same heuristic strategy at the same time; and

- educates stakeholders about the skills, mind-sets, and heart-sets behind collaboration.

In the next chapter, I'll talk about another key role in the Interaction Method—that of recorder. The chapter will include a discussion of the concept of group memory and the importance of the physical environment of meetings, including such seemingly mundane things as the arrangement of chairs in the meeting room.

# Chapter 6

# Harness the Power of Group Memory

Dan, a senior manager at a large bank, was charged with launching a task force to explore ways to exploit the powers of the Internet and to make recommendations for investment in e-business solutions. Dan asked me to sit in on one of his initial meetings to observe and offer process suggestions. This was my first time working with Dan. He was not yet comfortable having someone else facilitate, so he ran the meeting himself. The venue was a boardroom with a large, oval mahogany table surrounded by leather armchairs on wheels. Dan sat at one end of the oval, with the ten task force members facing him around the table. I sat off to the side. My only pre-meeting intervention was to have a chart pad and easel placed near me.

Fifteen minutes into the session, many of the common meeting problems were in evidence. People were making the same comments, over and over. Many were confused about what exactly they were supposed to be discussing. At times, the conversation seemed to be going around in circles. At a break in the discussion, I asked if anyone would mind if I recorded the ideas being proposed, since I was getting confused. No one objected, and the rambling conversation soon began again. I stood up, took out my markers, and started to capture on the chart pad what was being said. Rather than just flipping the sheets of chart pad paper over the back of the easel, I tore them off, and, using masking tape, began mounting the sheets in sequence on one of the long walls of the conference room.

At first no one took much notice of what I was doing, but soon participants started pointing to the information on the walls or correcting what I was writing. "We already covered that point over there." "No, I meant 250, not 200." "What did we say about that? Oh yes, there it is on page three." "Let's continue with this list before jumping to a new topic."

As the expanse of paper was extended down the long wall of the boardroom, participants with their backs to it began rolling their chairs around to the opposite side of the table so they could read the record more clearly. Soon, the task force members had arranged themselves in a U-shape, around the two short ends and one long side of the conference table. Dan was still running the meeting, but he was also more actively intervening to ensure that I was capturing ideas accurately and that participants didn't move on before completing a task. The power of *group memory* was at work, without ever being formally introduced.

## The Power of Group Memory

In the field of collaborative action, I've found few ideas as powerful—yet as deceptively simple—as the concept of group memory. A *group memory* is a record of the ideas raised and decisions made at a meeting, written on large sheets of paper and posted in full view of group members. This display of a group's problem solving creates a working memory, which is useful both in the short term (during the meeting) and the long term (days, weeks, or even months later). The role of the recorder, as I mentioned in the previous chapter, is to capture the key ideas of group members, using their own words. The recorder can edit the contributions but should not paraphrase them, nor should he or she participate in the discussion while in role. It is the responsibility of group members to make sure their ideas have been recorded accurately.

Managers, leaders, and chairpeople typically employ some kind of recording in their meetings. In fact, the use of chart pads and markers has become quite popular. But few people understand the purpose or power of this activity. Many see the physical activity of writing on a chart pad with colored markers as so straightforward as to be trivial. Others abuse the practice. For example, some recorders try to control or manipulate the discussion by capturing only the ideas they like, rather than working as a servant of the group and recording whatever participants say. That's simply not an appropriate use of the concept of group memory.

When chart pads aren't employed, meeting leaders will often have a person take notes on notepaper or a laptop, with the intention of writing up "meeting minutes" later on. The concept of group memory, a real-time record of the meeting, is much more powerful, as we shall see in this chapter. The effectiveness of a meeting and the quality of collaboration will almost always improve if group memory is employed. In fact, when done correctly, this simple activity prevents a number of serious meeting problems. That's why I have designated the fifth principle of collaboration as: *Harness the power of group memory.*

In this chapter, I'll first explain where the concept of group memory came from. Then I'll show how key meeting problems are addressed by the effective use of group memory. Finally, I'll explain how group memory is made most effective when the physical meeting space is organized appropriately.

## Historical Roots

I first experienced the power of group memory when I first saw facilitation in action—at the Synectics creative problem-solving workshop I mentioned in the previous chapter. At that workshop, several chart pads were mounted at the front of the room on hooks, and comfortable chairs were arranged in a semicircle facing them. The meeting leader served as facilitator as well as recorder. It was quite clear to me then that the workshop leader's process of writing ideas on the chart pad paper helped to focus the group's discussion.

A year later, as I was researching problem-solving heuristics, I met Geoff Ball, the facilitator I mentioned, who was then working at the Stanford Research Institute in Palo Alto, California. Geoff, a member of the Augmented Human Research Center led by Doug Englebart, was experimenting with creating a protocol of a group's work using large sheets of newsprint taped to the wall. It was during conversations with Geoff, who had coined the phrase "explicit group memory," that I really began to realize the powerful effect of this seemingly simple process of recording ideas in front of a group.

Around this time, I was asked by Far West Laboratories, one of the regional research centers of the U.S. Department of Education, to plan and conduct a four-day design conference, or *charette*. The lab was relocating its offices to a warehouse in San Francisco's Mission District, and the purpose of the charette was to have community members collaboratively decide how space in the new facility could be used to serve the needs of both the lab and the neighborhood.

This charette, which was conducted on a huge, unfinished, and unheated floor of the warehouse, was my first experience designing and facilitating a large consensus-building process. I was learning and inventing on the spot. I had all of the principles of collaborative action in play. I remember how useful, even comforting, the tools of recording were: the sheets of newsprint, the masking tape, the colored markers. As the days progressed, the work of the small groups was posted on the walls next to the revised sketches of the architects who were working with us. In this way, the stakeholders from the community could see clearly that their input was being taken seriously and that the emerging design would reflect their ideas.

Since the charette agenda called for several small groups to work in parallel, I had conducted a preconference workshop to train volunteer facilitators and recorders. That session, which was my first involving training others in facilitation and recording, was attended by Geoff and a talented graphic artist named David Sibbet. David went on to experiment with creating images of a group's work in words and drawings on long, horizontal sheets of newsprint. He and others have transferred this technique through workshops and launched the related profession of *graphic facilitation*.

## How Group Memory Prevents Common Meeting Problems

This section shows how the effective use of group memory prevents nine typical meeting problems.

### 1. Repetition and "Wheel Spinning"

Repetition is one of the most common meeting problems. It may be that one individual repeats the same ideas endlessly. Most people can retain seven, plus or minus two, separate pieces of information in their short-term memories. So what happens when a person comes to a meeting with more than nine items he wants to discuss? The person will tend to keep repeating the ideas, because he can't remember if he has brought them up already. Or he may just be worried that the group has forgotten about them. In other cases, participants who have not been listening closely or just like to hear themselves talk may repeat ideas that have already been clearly stated.

By using group memory, participants' ideas are recorded in front of the group. This can be a great relief to them—they can then let the ideas go because the ideas are out there on paper. The group memory will "remember" them. By scanning the record of the meeting, participants can easily see where their ideas, as well as everyone else's, have been documented.

Group memory also greatly helps the facilitator prevent repetition. When someone repeats an idea, the facilitator can intervene by saying, "Sally, I think we've recorded that idea already. It's there in blue on page three of the group memory, and again in green on page five. Anything else you want to add? If not, let's move on."

### 2. Lack of a Level Playing Field

In many meetings, there are significant differences among participants in terms of perceived status, authority, or expertise. Where these differences exist, participants may come to a meeting concerned about whether their ideas will be heard and taken seriously. The use of group memory helps to build a level playing field and address issues of diversity. Using this technique, the recorder captures all ideas in the words of the speaker without judgment— without trying to decide if the idea is worth considering. The recorder does not and should not serve as a gatekeeper for ideas. Everyone's contribution is captured and given equal weight.

While a typical meeting note taker may also capture all ideas on a notepad or a laptop without judgment, participants are unaware of this. They can't see it being done. So having a note taker does little to improve the tenor of the meeting. With group memory, on the other hand, the very act of recording in front of the group helps to create a safe environment in which all ideas are accepted and legitimized.

### 3. Associating Ideas With People

Associating an idea too closely with a specific participant can create a barrier to agreement. If you are angry with or dislike a certain participant, you may find yourself rejecting an idea just because he or she offered it—even if the idea has merit. Without a visual record of an idea, participants may only remember the idea by associating it with a particular person. With group memory, by contrast, all ideas are recorded on paper without attribution in front of the group, so there is an increased likelihood that group members will forget who said what and that each contribution will be "owned" by the group as a whole. The group memory is a record of the *group's* work, and the information it contains tends to become depersonalized.

### 4. Loss of Focus

Groups lose focus easily. It's hard for people to keep concentrating on the same problem, using the same process, at the same time. The use of group memory can help, since participants must sit in a semicircle in order to see both the recording and each other. This concave shape acts like a lens, focusing the light of the group in one direction. The facilitator can further narrow the attention of the group by pointing to or circling an item on the group memory. "Let's keep clarifying *this* item before we move on to the next, OK?" she might say. That is a very strong and useful intervention to make to regain focus.

### 5. The Limitation of Words

A note taker using a laptop to capture ideas in a meeting is limited to expressing those ideas in words. He or she can't quickly draw in sketches, graphics, tables, arrows to connect ideas, and so forth. A recorder using chart pad paper doesn't have this limitation. With the cheap, expandable display area of group memory, a recorder can capture and present a great deal of information easily. He or she can draw diagrams, present figures, make lists, and visually indicate connections between ideas. This ability to translate ideas into pictures helps greatly to clarify ideas and build agreement. In addition, the display medium is the record of the meeting. The sheets can be moved to other walls or surfaces during the meeting and, later, transported to wherever the follow-up meeting is to be held.

The sheer amount of information that can be displayed by sheets of paper taped to the four walls of a meeting room is staggering—sometimes overwhelming. You can display more information more cheaply with markers and chart pads taped around a room than with any electronic meeting support system I have yet seen. Using chart pad paper also helps participants make mental connections and relationships—it lets them remember key ideas or conversations just by visually scanning the room. And using small, sticky pieces of paper like Post-it™ Notes allows you to organize and reassemble information in infinite ways.

### 6. Information Overload

Many problem-solving methods involve multiple steps. For example, one often-used approach requires brainstorming a list of ideas, then clarifying each item, eliminating duplicates, and, finally, rank ordering or grouping the items. It would be ridiculous to ask people to keep track of all of this information in their heads. The task simply couldn't be accomplished without some means of recording and displaying information. Since most collaborative problem-solving efforts require the heuristic application of multistepped agreement-building methods, some kind of graphic recording is absolutely essential.

### 7. Disruption by Latecomers

Group memory handles another common meeting problem— dealing with latecomers. Rather than having to stop a meeting to explain to someone who comes in late what has been discussed, a facilitator can reasonably request that the person sit down, read what has been recorded, and join in when he or she feels caught up. The latecomer can easily review the group memory to see what has happened and to figure out what's happening at the moment.

The facilitator can also use the group memory at a break as an aid to answering any questions the latecomer may have.

## 8. Vague or Misunderstood Agreements

It's not uncommon in meetings for participants to walk out of the room with very different understandings of agreements reached or of who is going to do what next. Each person thinks he or she understands perfectly well, but everyone may return to a follow-up meeting and discover that they each had their own interpretation. It's thus essential that agreements and "next steps" lists be captured in writing during the meeting.

The act of recording emerging agreements on chart pad paper in front of all parties is a powerful facilitative intervention for surfacing and avoiding potential misunderstandings and for cementing decisions. If, for example, the members of your team see charted before them a list of tasks and associated deadlines with their names attached, and they must look everyone in the eye and confirm these agreements, they have very little wiggle room. When the original chart pads are brought back into the room around the due date, there is absolutely no place to hide!

## 9. The Failure of Memory

In the weeks following a meeting, participants will often forget much of what occurred—particularly if the meeting was long or they were mentally engaged only intermittently. They may remember some key agreements but forget other productive conversations. Group memory preserves all relevant information.

Group memory creates a lasting record of not only the content and results of a meeting, but also the process of problem solving used to achieve those results. What makes group memory so powerful is that you experience it being created; you see where words and diagrams are being placed on a page; you watch as a phrase is crossed out and replaced by another; you witness agreements being circled or highlighted; you notice items being misspelled or pages being torn in haste. When you review the sheets of newsprint days, weeks, or even months later, you often have a visceral, almost kinesthetic memory of what it was like to be in that room in that meeting at that point in time. Some cognitive psychologists believe that the brain stores traces of the *experience* of seeing and hearing, not records of the actual images and sounds. Remembering may, in fact, be literally "re-membering" or reconstructing the original experience. The handwriting, diagrams, squiggles, and even misspellings all serve as "memory hooks" to remind you of the original event. Then, after the meeting, these handwritten chart pad sheets can be reduced to 8½-by-11-inch sheets of paper or digital files using several types of currently available technologies.

At some point, the information captured in group memory may need to be translated into typewritten text, which can easily be processed and communicated. But something powerful may be lost if the informal, fuzzier, and messier form of recording is eliminated from the process. For example, it's now possible to create a kind of group memory by typing ideas on a laptop and projecting the resulting text in front of a group in real time. With this technology, though, the recorder can only display a limited amount of information before he or she must scroll it out of view. Even more important, I've found that in meetings where this technology is used, participants start focusing on misspellings and other details rather than on the ideas themselves. Writing and drawing by hand allows for a kind of shorthand notation and lack of specificity that is supportive of the tenderness and tentativeness of ideas in formation. Especially in heuristic collaborative problem solving, thoughts may emerge ill formed and ill defined. A group needs to be careful not to stunt those ideas by trying to be too precise too quickly—as seems to happen when ideas are typed on a display in front of a group. Just as I found it easier to draft my partially formed thoughts for this book using paper and a pen (even though my next step was to refine them on my laptop), a handwritten group memory may well be the most appropriate technology for capturing and preserving the thoughts of a group engaged in creative problem solving. If, on the other hand, the task of the group requires precision and accuracy—as in preparing a budget or editing a final draft of a document—it can be very helpful to use a computer projection system to display and manipulate that information in real time.

## The Power of Changing the Physical Environment

The physical environment of a meeting room, especially the placement of chairs, has a powerful impact on a meeting. The conventional seating arrangement for many meetings includes chairs arranged around a conference table. This enclosed shape tends to focus participants' energy on one another, which often increases interpersonal conflict. In this setup, people are facing each other, rather than a common task. The circle is a great form for a dinner party or a dialogue, but not for a problem-solving session.

By contrast, a semicircular seating arrangement opens up the space and, like a lens, focuses the energy of a group in a common direction (toward the group memory), while still permitting eye contact among participants. There's something about the curvature of the semicircle that conveys togetherness and teamwork. It enables participants to address their comments towards the facilitator and the neutral ground of the group memory, as well as to each other.

So one of the most powerful interventions you can make is to arrange the seating before the meeting begins. Get rid of the solid mahogany table, find some narrow movable tables, and position them so that the open end of the "U" faces a flush, blank wall. Even better, get rid of the tables altogether and simply arrange the chairs in a semicircle. Yes, there will be howls of protest. Participants have become accustomed to hiding behind a solid barrier (and there are times when they need a place to put a laptop and papers). However, when participants enter the rearranged room, they will know they are in for a different kind of meeting, one in which the focus will not be on one another or on the meeting leader, but on a common task.

As a leader, once you get the focus off yourself in this way, you will improve your meetings dramatically. There is a strong relationship between the effectiveness of a work group and the seating pattern. You can see this most easily in collaborative processes in which several small groups work simultaneously in different rooms. If you circulate around the breakout rooms, you may observe that the most productive, focused discussions occur where the chairs are arranged in a relatively neat, tight semicircle without empty seats (which function like "energy holes"), and where the facilitator can walk into the space in front of the chairs. Where participants are scattered around the room or even circled up around a table with the facilitator forced to the periphery, it's likely that the conversation is rambling and the task is not getting accomplished. While the quality of facilitation has the most impact on a group's productivity, the effectiveness of the recording and the accompanying seating arrangement are also very important.

The physical environment for successful collaborative action requires more than just a semicircular seating arrangement, however. Ideally, you need extensive, flat wall surfaces on which paper can be pinned or taped; lighting that washes the walls; comfortable chairs on wheels; and, for long meetings, some natural light. If you are going to use tables, it's best to have narrow, easily moveable tables that can be moved into appropriately sized U-shapes. It's also helpful to have access to phones, local area networks, projection systems for video and computer, and audio and video conferencing equipment.

Most meeting rooms are not designed to support effective collaboration. Usually you have to reconfigure them by rearranging tables and chairs and creating flat surfaces on which to mount the chart pad paper. My colleagues and I have made some memorable room transformations over the years. We once removed paintings from the walls of the Museum of Modern Art in New York, for example, so that we could post newsprint for a group memory. We've also taped chart pads to the shark tanks at Marine World, tipped folded tables on end to create smooth surfaces in paneled board rooms, and mounted paper on the picture windows of mansions and executive retreat rooms. If you have the will, there is a way to reconfigure any room so that group memory can be used.

Even after all these years, I always feel a little anxious before facilitating a meeting with a new group in a new location. It's safe to assume that no matter how much you specify the setup in advance, the meeting room will not be arranged the way you want it. The chairs will be oriented in the wrong direction or set up around a large table, the walls will be paneled, or the semicircle of chairs will be too close to or too far away from the display wall. In any case, I know I always need to arrive early to set up banks of paper on the wall for the group memory and to chart the agenda and desired outcomes. The process of rearranging the chairs is familiar and comforting to me, and allows me to transform the meeting environment. Such janitorial activities actually help me to relax, and enable me to set up the meeting for success. At the root of this intervention is the power of the group memory.

## Conclusion

Just like facilitation, the practice of recording what is happening in a meeting on chart pad paper has become increasingly popular. Most conference rooms are equipped with easels, chart pads, tape, and colored markers. Rather than flipping chart pad sheets over the back of the stand, most recorders now tape completed sheets around the room, thereby creating a group memory. But, just as with facilitation, the practice of recording can be abused or trivialized. It's not uncommon for a manager to grab the markers and further control the process of a meeting. Especially as new recording technologies are being introduced in face-to-face as well as virtual meetings, it is important to keep in mind the fundamental purposes and functions of group memory—namely, to capture all ideas accurately and depersonalize them, prevent repetition and wheel spinning, focus the energy of the group, encourage pictures as well as words, support multistepped problem-solving processes, nail down agreements, and create an accessible record of the process as well as the content. All this from markers and newsprint!

So, there you have it, the five principles of collaboration: involve the relevant stakeholders, build consensus phase by phase, design a process map, designate a process facilitator, and harness the power of group memory. So simple and straightforward, yet so powerful. Next, we'll look at how to put all five of these principles into practice together. We'll begin by looking at leadership and how your style of leadership will need to change if you are going to foster collaboration effectively in your group, organization, or community.

# Part III

# Putting It All Together

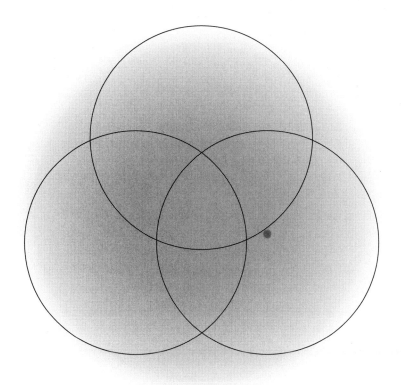

# Chapter 7

# Facilitative Leadership

Leaders have a profound effect on the cultures of their organizations and communities. The support of leadership is essential if an organization or community is to build a collaborative environment and implement the five principles of collaboration.

These truths became clear to me when I facilitated a retreat in Northern California for a city manager and his staff. The retreat was designed, in part, to allow the staff to surface problems that affected everyone, and then to collaboratively develop solutions to those problems. In the preretreat planning session, the city manager expressed considerable enthusiasm and support for this kind of collaborative problem solving. During the retreat, we hit a snag when the participants had some difficulty brainstorming potential problems to work on. They seemed to feel very inhibited and couldn't come up with many good examples.

What was needed at that point was for the city manager to assure his staff that it was OK to be honest about any problems that existed, be they small or large, and to encourage them to think openly and "outside the box." Instead, the manager stood up and delivered one of the most uncollaborative leadership messages I've ever witnessed. "You are a talented group," he began. "I hired you because you are good problem solvers, and I have given you the authority to deal with the problems of your own departments. So if you have a problem for us to work on, it had better be a serious problem or else you are not doing your job."

Here I was, asking the staff to brainstorm—to throw out ideas without concern for their value—while their manager was telling them they were in trouble if they did! It was a memorable illustration of how *not* to foster collaboration.

Harnessing the power of collaborative action requires a different model of leadership than the classic "command-and-control" model, in which the leader solves problems, makes decisions, and issues orders unilaterally. Indeed, the old model is antithetical to building a collaborative culture.

To harness the power of collaborative action, you must become a *facilitative leader*. A facilitative leader is one who engages relevant stakeholders in solving problems collaboratively and works to build a more collaborative culture in his or her organization or community. A facilitative leader has the usual positional power to act unilaterally, but chooses instead to work with others when appropriate to find win-win solutions to important issues.

The five principles in Part II of this book provided guidance on designing and facilitating a process of collaboration. Each of the five principles contains a message for you as a leader. *Stakeholder involvement* suggests that you as a decision maker engage other stakeholders in solving problems and making decisions. *Consensus building* suggests that you work for agreement on a definition of the problem and for alignment on a vision before advocating solutions. *Process design* suggests that part of your role as a leader is to convene, promote, and support collaborative action throughout your organization or community, and insist on clear, well-designed process maps for each collaborative effort. *Facilitation* suggests that you get out of the way and let someone else facilitate your meetings. And *group memory* suggests that you prevent common meeting problems by getting someone to create a record of your meetings on chart pad paper.

This chapter builds on the leadership messages of those five principles and sets forth a practical model for facilitative leadership. It looks at the role of leadership in supporting collaborative action in a group, organization, or community. The chapter is addressed primarily toward leaders and decision makers. But whether or not you are currently a manager in your organization or an elected or appointed official in your community, you most likely have opportunities to lead and influence the people around you. So, no matter what your title, you can play an important leadership role in assisting your group, organization, or community to learn to be more collaborative.

This chapter focuses on four skill sets essential to facilitative leadership:

- Choosing when and how much collaboration is appropriate

- Being consistent in your words and actions

- Supporting and promoting collaborative action

- Creating a collaborative culture

## Choosing When and How Much Collaboration Is Appropriate

Many leaders, once they understand the advantages of collaborative action, believe that all decisions should be made by consensus. Sometimes they even abdicate their responsibilities as leaders completely and become passive members of their team. Obviously, that's *not* what we advocate! Collaboration needn't be used on every minor decision and problem, and it's not a way for you to avoid your duties as a manager and decision maker. As a facilitative leader, you retain all of your decision-making responsibilities. The art of facilitative leadership, then, involves making conscious choices about how much collaboration is appropriate for each decision. After all, there are many levels of involvement between making a decision unilaterally and delegating it to an individual or group below you. To help clarify these levels of involvement, my colleagues at Interaction Associates and I developed the model in Figure 19.

In this figure, the horizontal axis represents "level of involvement" and the vertical axis represents "level of ownership." As you move up the circles from left to right, the decision-making processes require more stakeholder involvement and inspire in stakeholders a greater sense of ownership of the decision. Let's examine briefly each of these decision-making options.

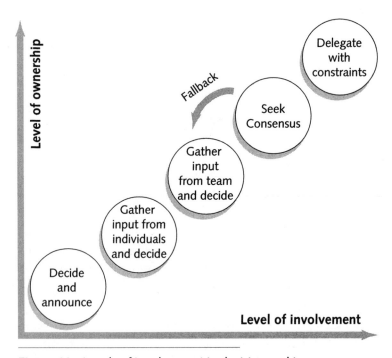

**Figure 19:** Levels of involvement in decision making

## Decide and Announce

As a facilitative leader, you don't need to make decisions by consensus all the time. It's often completely appropriate for you to
make a decision with little or no input and then announce your
decision to the rest of your group, organization, or community.
These are the times when strength and will are necessary—when
you have to bite the proverbial bullet and make a decision. It
may be that the situation is something of an emergency and requires immediate action. There's no time to get people together
to talk about it. Or, the decision may involve being consistent
with your agreed-upon core values and strategies. For example,
you might have to state strongly: "We will implement our stated
policy of seeking diversity in all hiring decisions." There may
even be times when, paradoxically, you have to be authoritarian
about being collaborative: "I insist that this issue be resolved collaboratively."

The great advantage of the decide-and-announce option, of
course, is speed. You can make the decision quickly and begin to
implement it immediately. The disadvantages of this approach
read like the arguments *for* collaboration:

- Stakeholders may have the power to block your decision, or
  at least resist its implementation.

- The decision won't be as good without the input of others.

- It may take a long time to sell your decision to stakeholders,
  and you may meet with resistance from others just because
  they weren't consulted.

- You've made a commitment to involve stakeholders in
  decisions that affect their lives and your "decide-and-
  announce" decision appears to violate that commitment.

If you have to make a decide-and-announce decision, try to
frame your decision in its context, explaining the underlying rationale for it and how the criteria you used are consistent with

the established vision, mission, values, and strategies of your organization or community.

### Gather Input from Individuals and Decide

Stakeholder involvement, as we've learned, is one of the key principles of collaboration. But it's possible to involve stakeholders without having them meet face-to-face. Sometimes it may be appropriate, and more efficient, to contact key stakeholders individually to gather input from them before making your decision. That way, the stakeholders will feel included, and you'll have the benefit of their advice. This option works best for those decisions that are clearly yours to make, but for which input may be helpful to you—as in the case of personnel issues, for example.

But be careful. If you choose to ignore stakeholders' advice, they may feel resentful and less likely to be direct with you the next time you seek their opinions. During your conversations with them, try to be clear that you are not seeking consensus, but that you do value their input. If possible, explain the criteria you will be using to make your decision, and let them know when and how they will be informed of it.

### Gather Input from the Team and Decide

There is something powerful about discussing ideas openly in a group. Everyone hears the same ideas raised and has a chance to consider and respond to those ideas, and everyone learns how others feel about an issue. As a decision maker, you have the option, short of direct consensus building, to convene a meeting and solicit input on a decision that you will make later on your own. Perhaps the decision is too trivial (e.g., the location of the new copier) or too pressing (e.g., whether to bid on a specific contract) to take the time to work for consensus. However, you may believe it's important for participants to hear each other's ideas and to witness that you as decision maker have heard them.

The one danger with this option is that the group may clearly favor a particular course of action, and you may choose later to do something different. If this happens, you may bring about greater resistance than if you had just consulted people individually. So, if your mind is already made up, don't hold an information-gathering session. And when you do choose this option, you may want to inform stakeholders that you reserve the right to disagree with them, and that you will base your decision not only on their ideas but on external factors as well. You should also let participants know when you will be making your decision and how you will inform them of it.

## Seek Consensus

By now, the definition and benefits of consensus should be clear. The five principles of collaboration I presented (stakeholder involvement, consensus building, process design, facilitation, and group memory) all advocate for the advantages of this decision-making option. And remember: There is a clear fallback if consensus can't be reached. You, as formal decision maker, must approve of the final decision. You can't be outvoted. If you disagree with an emerging consensus decision, you can just say so, and (unless the group can convince you otherwise) that option will be abandoned.

This is a good place to stress an important point: It takes personal strength and maturity to be a good facilitative leader. Making a decision by consensus involves being open and honest, and therefore exposed and vulnerable. Your problem-solving processes and the content of your thinking are visible for everyone to observe. People will see your humanity—your heuristic mistakes as well as your intelligent solutions. A more autocratic leader can hide behind his or her office door, go through the messiness of human problem solving, and then present a proposal in its final, polished form. A facilitative leader must feel comfortable revealing what he or she knows and doesn't know and not be afraid of looking "stupid." Fortunately, the benefits of being a collaborative leader are tremendous. Being collaborative builds teamwork, strengthens relationships and trust, and transfers skills and knowledge to your team members. It's worth the risks.

Many leaders fear that if they opt for a facilitated, consensus-based process, they will end up being the lone voice in support of a particular option. I have rarely seen this happen. If the issues are complex and several reasonable options exist, usually more than one person will advocate for each solution. If you get to a point at which the group is divided between two or more options and time is running out, often your direct reports will be more than willing to pass the decision back to you. They will understand better how difficult the decision is and how hard it would be to reach consensus, and they will know you have heard all the different points of view. In fact, the members of your team may be relieved to have you make the final decision.

Whether or not consensus is reached, you will advance the cause of collaborative action by striving for it. If consensus is reached, your decision will be based on this consensus, and stakeholders will feel empowered and proud to have taken part in the process. If consensus isn't reached, you will have demonstrated your commitment to collaborative decision making, and your team will most likely support whatever you decide.

## Delegate Decisions with Constraints

As a leader, one of the best ways to build a collaborative culture in your organization or community is to get out of the way and turn the responsibility for making a decision over to the appropriate stakeholders. If you have built alignment on the important issues of vision, mission, values, and strategy, you should be able to trust others to make good decisions.

You can do several things to ensure successful delegation. First, be clear about the boundaries of the decision—in other words, the constraints in terms of dollars, time, resources, etc. Be explicit about the charge or task and any criteria that an acceptable solution must meet. Also, if your formal approval of the decision is necessary, insist on reviewing a map of the decision-making process to ensure that there are checkpoints at the end of each phase. In this way, you, as a stakeholder, can be part of the agreement-building process and approve the group's definition and analysis of the problem before they work to find solutions. Delegation does not mean abdication. With good process design, you can efficiently and effectively support a group to address an issue while still being part of the final decision.

## Which Option to Use When

So, how do you know when to use which decision-making option? It's impossible to give a precise answer to that question, because so much depends on the context and the specifics of the decision you are trying to make. But you can weigh a number of factors to help you decide:

- **Stakeholder Buy-In.** How much do key stakeholders need to be involved so that they can confidently support the implementation of the decision?

- **Available Time.** How much time can be spent making the decision?

- **Importance of the Decision.** How important is the issue to the people in your organization or community?

- **Needed Information.** Who has information or expertise that can contribute to a quality decision?

- **Capability.** How capable and experienced are people in operating as decision makers or as a decision-making team?

- **Teamwork Opportunity.** What is the potential value of using this opportunity to create a stronger team?

So, to review, one skill necessary for facilitative leadership is the ability to make conscious choices about the appropriate level of involvement required for each issue or decision as it arises. As the level of trust grows in your group, organization, or community, your "followers" will become more willing to have you make decisions on their behalf. And you, in turn, will feel more trust in delegating decisions to them.

## Making Your Words and Actions Congruent

What you do as a leader has as much effect as—if not more than—what you say. If you want to build a more collaborative culture, you must begin by acting collaboratively. Your words and actions must be congruent. How you run your meetings, how you interact with your top team, even which pronouns you use ("we" vs. "I") all send a message to your people about whether or not you are serious about teamwork and collaboration—whether you really intend to change how your group or organization works, or whether your actions are window dressing. When you first start being more facilitative in your leadership style, your symbolic acts, especially your uncharacteristic symbolic acts, may be the most powerful tools you have.

### Uncharacteristic Symbolic Acts

*Uncharacteristic symbolic acts* are just what they sound like—actions you take or decisions you make as a leader that startle people into realizing that you intend to change the way you lead. I remember two great examples of symbolic acts from our consulting work with Jack Telnak, head of the design division at Ford Motor Company.

At the time, Jack realized he needed to communicate the message that truck designers were just as important to the company as car designers. (In fact, trucks were much more profitable to produce.) As a prerogative of his position, Jack got to drive home a different vehicle every evening in order to check out the competition. All of the employees in the division watched to see what kind of machine was stationed in Jack's parking space. He had traditionally chosen sexy foreign cars like Jaguars and Porsches. Imagine the impact and the symbolic message when, for a change, a series of different model trucks was parked where only luxury automobiles had been before. By this simple symbolic act, Jack sent a powerful message to his employees: Truck design is as important to us as car design.

Jack made another symbolic move when he initiated the collaborative effort I mentioned in Chapter 4, to shorten the design cycle for new vehicles. Jack had come to realize that the design process was taking far too long, and that something radical had to be done to get the other senior vice presidents to realize it as well. In their meetings together, the senior VPs always worked hard to make their own divisions look good and to cover up any problems. At a key meeting, then, Jack stood up and publicly "shot himself in the foot." "Our design and engineering process is taking us too long," he said, "and here is how my design division is contributing to the problem." Jack went on to list ways in which the design process was being drawn out longer than absolutely necessary. But Jack continued, "I don't think we are the only ones. What do you think you all contribute to this mess?" Then, following Jack's uncharacteristic lead, other VPs began to admit their responsibility for the problem. At that point, Jack suggested forming a cross-functional committee to analyze the problem and return with some recommendations. With that one uncharacteristic act, he launched what turned out to be a critical and very successful collaborative effort in process redesign.

## Being Facilitative in Meetings

Systems change only through the constant reinforcement and demonstrated success of the desired behaviors, attitudes, and values. Your task as a facilitative leader is to demonstrate the power of collaborative action whenever and wherever you can. One important venue is your own meetings. Where you sit, how you set up the room, who facilitates the meeting, and how and when you participate all send important clues to the members of your team about whether or not you are interested in open and honest discussion and true collaboration.

One powerful symbolic act is to simply rearrange the chairs—to get rid of your conference table, arrange the chairs in a U-shape, and tack flipcharts to the walls. The rearrangement of the meeting space will communicate that the focus is not on you as the leader, but on some common task.

Ask someone else to facilitate—or at least record—your meetings. Having someone else facilitate, as I've discussed, gets you out of the dual role of process leader and content leader, and removes from you the burden of having to worry about meeting logistics. You'll find that the constructive give-and-take with the facilitator is very liberating, allowing you to focus on the issues and advocate for your ideas, without dominating the group in your enthusiasm.

You can also demonstrate the power of collaboration by learning to be a good participant in a meeting—by practicing effective facilitative interventions and preventions, even when you are not facilitating. Facilitative preventions include such actions as getting agreement on outcomes, the agenda, meeting roles, decision making, and ground rules before leaping into the substantive discussion. A simple facilitative request such as, "Let's agree on how we are going to address this issue before we leap in," can be very effective and models good collaborative behavior. Then, during the meeting you can demonstrate facilitative interventions by, for example, asking open-ended questions, redirecting questions rather than always answering them, listening and paraphrasing, and refocusing the discussion when participants get off track.

## Supporting and Promoting
## Collaborative Action

It's been something of a cliché to say that managers do things right; leaders do the right things. We would say that *facilitative leaders get the right people to collaborate on the right things.* Many people in leadership positions feel responsible for producing answers to organizational issues themselves. But you will rarely get it right by yourself, and even if you do, making decisions on your own is disempowering for your organization.

Your role as a facilitative leader is to focus the energies of your organization on the most strategic issues, not to solve them yourself. Your role is to get the right people working on the right problems, with the right processes and resources. To do this, there are several powerful tools at your disposal: you can convene, promote, design, charter, and support collaborative processes. Let's look at each of these tools separately.

## Convene

One of the most powerful ways in which you can use your positional power as a leader is to convene. You can say, "Please come to a meeting I'm holding to address this important issue," and people will come—particularly if those people are your subordinates. That's one of the great features of a hierarchy—clarity about who has more decision-making power than whom. But even if the invitees are not your subordinates, the prestige of your office or your organization may be plenty of incentive to attract the people you want to come to a specific meeting. Sometimes just publishing a list of the other invitees can entice some people to come—people who don't want to be left out of something important.

Former President Jimmy Carter uses his position as former president of the United States very effectively to apply nonadversarial processes to address some of the world's most pressing problems. Using the venue of the Carter Center in Atlanta, Carter has for more than a decade been convening meetings to address such issues as Latin American debt and U.S. competitiveness. Carter sometimes will invite other international figures and former presidents to co-convene with him, to avoid any appearance of bias. He often uses professional facilitators or mediators to run these meetings. He invites participants to put aside prepared speeches and work with him informally and off-the-record to explore new solutions to intractable problems.

The format of these collaborative, facilitated work sessions is often new to the world leaders who attend, but, as I have witnessed, Carter's own modeling of facilitative behaviors and his active promoting of the values of openness and cooperation have been enough to bring together the right people to address issues in new, more constructive ways. Carter has clearly found that he can be more effective by applying collaborative processes than by trying to advocate for his own solutions.

### Promote

As President Carter has demonstrated, convening is only the first step you must take as a facilitative leader. Next, you must use your position to promote the power of collaborative action, to advocate for addressing a given problem cooperatively, rather than adversarially. Instead of trying to sell stakeholders on your solution to a problem, you need to invite them to join you in a collaborative process. You can use your position to promote collaborative action and, like a master in judo, focus the energy of the group on the right problem by means of a well-designed collaborative process. Furthermore, you can invite the participants to work with you to design the process itself. You can use the full moral force of your role as a leader to promote—or even present as a condition for your participation—the values of teamwork, inclusion, and collaboration.

Alex Plinio used this intervention effectively during the first meeting of stakeholders he convened at the beginning of the Newark Collaboration Group. At a strategic moment, Alex jumped in with an impassioned plea for the creation of a public-private partnership and the initiation of a collaborative, long-range planning process. He invited participants to join him in a self-selected process design group to explore how this might be done. Convene, advocate for collaboration, and then model facilitative behaviors by working with key stakeholders to design a planning process collaboratively: Alex Plinio demonstrated all these important practices of facilitative leadership in this one critical meeting in Newark.

## Design

Groups can tolerate only a certain level of ambiguity and chaos before a situation becomes dysfunctional. It would be intolerable in most cases for a leader to say, "I don't know what our strategy will be and I don't even know how we are going to develop one." However, it is acceptable, and often advisable, for a leader to say, "I don't know exactly what our final strategy will be, but here is the process by which we are going to build that strategy together." It's a question of degrees of freedom. You can and must, as a facilitative leader, be open-ended about responses to critical problems, turning the issues back to your organization to solve. But you also must insist on clear process maps for getting from here to there. People need to know when and how they will be involved. You, as a leader, need to know who is responsible for managing a process, who is going to be involved, and when the process will be completed. A process map, as we have seen, is a powerful tool for focusing the energies of your organization or community in a manageable collaborative effort. It's a way to reduce ambiguity but still keep the content of a decision open until it has been fully discussed by all relevant stakeholders.

So one of the levers you have as a facilitative leader is to require that a process map be designed for each important collaborative effort and that the key stakeholders, including you, agree to the map, with its milestones and deliverables, before the substantive discussions begin. Process maps are tools for ensuring that collaborative processes are open, visible, and inclusive before such efforts progress too far.

## Charter

Typically, a core team or task force forms the center of a collaborative project. The first phase of many efforts involves assembling the team and agreeing on the work plan, including the process map. It's important for you, as a facilitative leader, to also require that the team work with you to develop and agree to an explicit charter before work begins. A charter should clarify such issues as shared and meaningful purpose, specific and challenging goals, clear roles, common and collaborative approach, and complementary skills and resources. (See page 226 in Additional Models.) It allows you to be sure that the right problem is being addressed by the right people, in the right way, even though you may only be involved in the process at a few checkpoints.

### Support

To guarantee the success of a collaborative project once it's chartered and launched, you must actively support it. Your support as a leader can be crucial. Just showing up at approval meetings can have a powerful impact, demonstrating that the project is important and worthy of your valuable time. Obviously, your facilitative behaviors at these meetings can also reinforce the collaborative culture—you should listen more than speak, be respectful and appreciative of the effort that has been made, and contribute your own thoughts, as appropriate. You can also support a project by clearing the way through bureaucratic hurdles and making timely decisions that reinforce and speed up a project.

General Electric's "work out" process is a good example of leaders effectively supporting and resourcing a collaborative effort. In this process, decision makers and relevant stakeholders are assembled in one place with a limited amount of time. After prioritizing a list of key issues, work groups are formed with the charge of returning in a few hours with some recommendations. While the senior decision makers may not be involved in the subgroups, they return in person to listen to the reports and make decisions on the spot. It's clear from their presence and actions that the process is "for real" and that the work groups' recommendations will be acted upon.

You can also provide essential support for a project in more traditional ways, such as by providing release time, appropriate staffing and facilities, technology, process and technical assistance, skill development for the team, and funding for travel. Just designing a process and launching a task force is not enough. If you do not provide the project with the necessary resources, you might as well not get it started at all. Delivering critical support is another lever of the facilitative leader.

## Lead the Process of Cultural Change

If you want to build a collaborative environment, one capable of responding quickly in this rapidly changing world of global markets, then you must lead the process of cultural change. The cultures of groups and organizations are finely crafted systems—even in their dysfunctionality. Everyone colludes in maintaining the existing culture, even though many may complain vociferously. Everyone gets something out of the way things are, even if it is just predictability. No one is more essential for changing the culture than you, the leader.

Systemic change poses several significant challenges to you as a leader and agent of change. Much as people may complain about the old system, people are naturally afraid of change. The old and familiar is less threatening than the new and unpredictable. We have found that some of the most vocal critics of the old are also the most resistant to adopting new attitudes and behaviors. And change is difficult, time consuming, and sometimes painful. A system undergoing change may function more poorly for a while before it improves. For example, when you are learning to use a new or upgraded word-processing program, writing documents using the new program may take longer and be more difficult than using the old one—though after a while it should go faster and be more efficient. Similarly, when an autocratic system tries to become more collaborative, for a while things will seem to be a mess. There will seem to be more conflict rather than less as many of the old issues bubble to the surface and as everyone wants to be involved in everything. It takes a tremendous amount of courage and conviction to lead your system through such a change. When your organization or community hits a rough spot or crisis, there will be a strong tendency to fall back to the old ways of doing things. This is just when your commitment to and modeling of the new ways of doing things is most important. At these strategic moments, if you meet and work through the challenges collaboratively, you will have taken a great step in building a collaborative environment.

Most processes of cultural change progress through three phases. The first phase involves describing what exists today: accurately describing and acknowledging responsibility for the current norms, values, and behaviors. If the members of your organization don't recognize and understand the problem, they won't support the changes you want to make. You must participate with your team in a process of looking at how things actually work—not at your professed values and procedures, but at the unwritten rules of the road. To get at the current norms, we often ask the question this way: "If you were briefing a new member of your team about how to get along, how to fit in, what would you tell him or her about how to succeed—how not to rock the boat?" This often elicits smiles from the group and makes it OK to discuss things that are usually left unsaid.

Some of the norms and values may be positive—you may want to hold on to them. Others may be clearly destructive and not in keeping with the culture you would like to build. Your move as a facilitative leader is not only to make it comfortable for people to discuss the current culture but, more importantly, to acknowledge your role in having kept things the way they are. It's important to model openness and vulnerability, to be able to take responsibility for how you have colluded in maintaining the negative aspects of the current culture. If you can't do this yourself, you can't expect your direct reports to be brave enough to assume responsibility for their own role in the situation in your presence.

A good example of this kind of facilitative leadership style was modeled by the president of a hospital for which I did consulting work. Hospitals are notorious for the adversarial relationships that exist between administrators and physicians. In this particular hospital, everyone (president, physicians, administrators, nurses, even the board) complained about the institution's very autocratic, command-and-control culture and about the open warfare between the president and the division chiefs (who were physicians). After some coaching, the president openly admitted to his physician chiefs that in some ways he liked the fighting—it kept him in control and kept the chiefs from acquiring too much power. Besides, he could tolerate it because he only had to meet with them for two hours each month.

The division chiefs subsequently admitted that they also colluded in maintaining the system. By conducting one-on-one budget negotiations with the president instead of working collaboratively with other divisions, each chief thought he could make a better deal for his division and didn't have to worry about trade-offs with other divisions. Both the president and the division chiefs confessed to each other that they would have to give up these perceived benefits if they were to move to a more collaborative culture, one they agreed they needed in order to survive in a rapidly changing, competitive external environment.

The second phase of cultural change is often the easiest: agreeing on the new norms and behaviors toward which you want to move. If you have done a good job of uncovering what doesn't work in your current culture, you already have an idea of what you want in the new one. At this point, it's totally appropriate for you to use your positional power to advocate for values supporting collaborative action: respect for human dignity, and the right of appropriate stakeholder involvement. For many leaders, these values become nonnegotiable, absolute musts.

The third phase is the most difficult: adopting, modeling, and reinforcing the new values and behaviors to the point where they become the new norms. During the early period of this phase, the change process is most vulnerable. Everyone is watching for whether the change will stick—whether it's something that will last or just a passing fancy. The person they will watch the most will be you. If you are really trying to model the new, more collaborative behaviors, if you are "walking the talk," then the message will spread through the organization that a serious change is taking place. When you fail (as everyone does at some point), if you can laugh at yourself and acknowledge how difficult it is to change behaviors, this, too, will support the effort. Likewise, if you can acknowledge and celebrate change in others, you will reinforce the effort as a whole. It is particularly in times of crisis that organizational systems tend to snap back to old norms. During these time of stress, leaders must stay the course if they want the change to succeed.

## Conclusion

This chapter has touched on those leadership skill sets that most directly relate to supporting collaborative action and building collaborative cultures. (For an overview of our complete model of the seven practices of facilitative leadership, please refer to the Resources section.) The key message is that collaboration requires a new model of leadership—facilitative leadership—which is essential for building collaborative cultures in organizations and communities. Leaders have a profound impact on organizational cultures. Collaborative cultures can't be nurtured without the support and congruent actions of their leaders.

In the next chapter, I'll examine the links between culture and productivity, make the case for the effectiveness of collaborative organizations, and present some of the evidence that supports the assertion that collaborative environments are healthier, more satisfying places in which to work and live.

# Chapter 8

# Collaborative Organizations

I tend to be an abstract-to-concrete kind of thinker. I develop a somewhat intuitive theory first, and then work "downward" to see if it can be applied to specific situations. The opposite style of thinking—the more empirical approach—is to first observe lots of data and then work "upward" to generate a more abstract principle. That's definitely not my style. I arrived at the idea of facilitated meetings, for example, by starting with some general theories about human problem solving and the potential role of a process tool giver. The ideas just made sense to me, and I was excited to discover that they solved many practical meeting problems.

This same abstract-to-concrete thinking—and the same gut feeling of rightness—more recently convinced me of the validity of a concept I call the *collaborative organization*. It simply made sense to me that if collaborative problem solving works for one issue, it should work for most issues. And so I began to envision a new kind of organization, one that successfully institutionalizes all the principles of collaborative action. One in which the organizational structure, technology systems, reward systems, values, strategy, core skills, leadership, and culture all support and enable collaborative problem solving.

I must confess that this idea has generated a debate within my own organization about ends vs. means. Should collaboration be an end in and of itself, or is collaborative action simply a means to an end—a way to address specific problems? Should we promote the concept of a collaborative organization as a desired end state, or just continue to help clients apply collaborative problem solving to specific, defined issues? Many of my colleagues rightly point out that few of our customers are asking for help in building more collaborative organizations. Rather, most are coming with specific problems for which collaborative action may be a useful means of resolution. I'm convinced, however, that many CEOs will ultimately come to realize that building a collaborative organization is a necessary strategic response to a world that is ever more complex and uncertain.

In this chapter I'll talk about what happens when collaborative action is institutionalized throughout an organization or community. Specifically, I'll cover:

- the characteristics of an ideal collaborative organization (and some evidence that these characteristics already exist in some organizations);

- research that supports the effectiveness of collaborative organizations; and

- how to build collaborative organizations.

## Characteristics of Collaborative Organizations

In thinking about what a collaborative organization would look like, my colleagues and I started by assuming that it would embody the core values of respect for human dignity and commitment to collaboration, as well as the principles of stakeholder involvement, consensus building, process design, facilitation, and group memory. It was also clear that all aspects of the organization would need to be aligned—specifically, institutional structure, strategy, support technologies, reward systems, leadership styles, core skills, and corporate culture. What emerged from our thinking is the outline of a new organizational model.

What gives me such confidence in this emerging model is that it's also possible to arrive at it by studying what's actually happening in the field. As organizations today try to cope with forces in their environment, they are making changes that bring them closer to embodying the elements of the model. External forces include the increasing complexity of issues, greater uncertainty in the marketplace, customer demands for more quality and integrated services, and increased competition to reduce costs and speed up time-to-market. Internally, the workforce is demanding more involvement in decision making and access to information. So, there is evidence in innovative organizations today that the practices we recommend are being used to an ever-greater extent. I should note, however, that few (if any) organizations exhibit *all* of the characteristics of an ideal collaborative organization.

So, I'll describe our model for a collaborative organization in terms of seven key variables—organizational structure, information systems, reward systems, strategy, values, skills, and leadership/culture—and offer evidence that some organizations today have already begun to adopt collaborative practices in many of these areas.

## Organizational Structure

The ideal collaborative organization would be organized along several dimensions. Different hierarchies, teams, and multistakeholder task forces would coexist and would each be organized according to one particular dimension, such as function, product line, geography, and most importantly, customer. Each person would be a member of several different hierarchies and/or teams.

The result would be an organization that's fluid and adaptable—able to respond to external forces.

This kind of structure is quite complex, and could not be readily translated into an organizational chart. After all, it would look different depending on who's doing the looking at what point in time. For example, customers, suppliers, and partners would each have different mental images of the structure of such an organization, because they would each interact with different teams of people. So, while an organizational chart could be a valuable tool for assigning responsibility in a collaborative organization, it may be that many of them would have to be drawn up from different points of view to adequately describe how the organization works.

Also, each individual may appear in many places on the chart. If you worked in a collaborative organization, you might be the leader of one team, a member of another, and an occasional advisor to a third. For one team, you might report to a certain colleague; on another team, the two of you might be equal participants; and on another team, he or she might report to you. Clearly, collaborative problem-solving skills would be essential for navigating this web of relationships.

At Interaction Associates, we've developed a structure similar to the one described here, and we often find ourselves juggling multiple reporting relationships. At one point, for example, I was serving as chairman of the board as well as regional manager of our Cambridge office. In the latter position, I reported to our president—who technically reported back to me as chairman. I was also the leader or a member of several client-, practice-, and issue-focused teams. So, who was "in charge" depended very much on the context.

I have to admit that Interaction Associates has struggled with how best to organize and budget itself—whether by function, geography, line of service, core business processes, or customer. We have three offices around the United States in order to be geographically closer to our customers and provide a home base for our consultants, but we don't want to foster competition between offices. Our customers themselves are often global firms that request integrated services in several different locations. Meanwhile, we have two primary lines of business: learning (i.e., training) and consulting (i.e., designing and facilitating collaborative processes). The questions have been: How do we organize? Which dimension should we choose as our primary organizational category? Our answer for now is to organize along all three dimensions: geography, line of business, and customer. The result is that almost every employee is simultaneously a part of multiple teams and reports to multiple managers.

One thing we've learned is that, in a collaborative organization, positional authority means very little. People's individual credibility and competence, and the congruency between their stated beliefs and their actions, engender much more respect than their position or title. Having to resort to decide-and-announce decision making for an important decision is a sign that something is very wrong—that a manager has lost the confidence of his or her team or that the process of collaborative action has broken down. In thirty years, our board of directors has never had to make a decision by majority vote, and the only times I've had to make an executive decision I've done so as a fallback, after extensive attempts to reach consensus collaboratively have failed. Yes, it's essential to clarify who is ultimately responsible for a decision—who is the fallback decision maker—but in a collaborative organization, the fallback is rarely necessary.

In other organizations around the country, changes in structure have been going on for some time now. These organizations describe their structure as being "networked," "fishnet," "team based," "horizontal," "self-organizing," "open," "nonhierarchical," and/or "adaptable." Organizational charts are looking more like concentric circles, stars, overlays, and/or wiring diagrams. Organizations are becoming much flatter and leaner, with fewer middle managers. In some companies, the professional staff all have a common title, like "associate."

Professor Charles Heckscher of Rutgers University has been

studying the emergence of collaborative organizations since 1988. (See, for example, Heckscher & Donnellon, 1994, and Heckscher, 1991.) He has observed that as organizations take on increasing uncertainty and complexity, they must decouple resources from opportunities. In other words, they can't plan in advance what is going to be the best use of their uncommitted capital and human resources. Over the course of any given time period, unexpected opportunities may arise that require focusing resources on a new product opportunity, a new client, or a new market. You can't know in advance what those opportunities will be. The only way companies can adapt and respond is to organize dynamically around these new opportunities and resource them from uncommitted supplies of funds or people. This can only be accomplished through what Heckscher calls *collaborative linking mechanisms,* such as operating committees, councils, and project teams.

As a result, companies that are clinging to the traditional functional hierarchy are finding that they have to do more of their work in the parallel, informal organizational structure I described in Chapter 3 on consensus building. The number of ad hoc committees, groups, and teams is growing exponentially in response to the need to adapt, adjust, and address cross boundary issues more informally, more quickly, and more collaboratively. I think these companies will ultimately find that it doesn't make sense to cling to old structures at all—that all of their work can more effectively be accomplished with a flexible and adaptive team-based model.

This ability to dynamically organize and commit resources *depends on being able to work collaboratively.* The people who "own" the resources and the people who "own" the opportunities have to be able to make agreements and move quickly. Leaders can't hardwire these actions and decisions in advance. They have to create the guidelines and infrastructure—and be sure their people are trained in the appropriate skills—that will allow employees to react collaboratively and independently. This requires a very different kind of leadership, as we have seen, and a very different kind of organization.

### Information Systems

Almost by definition, the ideal collaborative organization would have to make use of sophisticated information systems. Fortunately, all the necessary technologies exist today and have been implemented in many organizations. In fact, it could be argued that technology itself is pushing organizations to be more open and collaborative with their employees. Let's examine five kinds of information systems that an ideal collaborative organization would utilize.

**Anybody-to-Anybody Communication.** In order for employees to form teams and address emerging opportunities quickly, each person in a collaborative organization would have to be able to communicate easily with everyone else in the organization, regardless of status, function, place, or time. The flow of communication would be free and unhindered by bureaucracy.

The advent of e-mail, voice mail, wireless phones, and the Internet have already made this vision a reality. We've become a wired (and wireless) nation and world. In many organizations, employees are already able to send messages to anyone in the organization. The ability to communicate easily is making intermediaries unnecessary. One of the main functions of middle managers has always been to control and enable the flow of information through an organization. Since the control of information is now essentially impossible and its free flow has been made possible, the need for middle management has decreased. Thus, organizations are becoming much flatter.

**Just-in-Time Access to Information.** The quality of collaborative decisions is dependent on the quality of information available and employees' access to that information. So, all employees in a collaborative organization would need to have access to relevant information about the business, its customers, and its external environment.

This, too, is already possible with existing technology. The development of local- and wide-area networks and high-speed and high-capacity servers has enabled large numbers of people to access the same information at the same time. Consider the airline reservation system, which allows agents and the general public to check on availability and book flights seamlessly and quickly. It's hard to imagine how a global business could operate without such information systems. While these systems were not created specifically to support collaboration, they certainly make it easier for employees and other stakeholders to have access to accurate, up-to-date information.

**Groupware.** In a truly collaborative organization, people would be able to collaborate with others who are separated geographically around the country and the world. Such an organization would make available to all of its employees the latest in groupware technologies, from teleconferencing and video conferencing systems to computer programs that support same-time and different-time collaboration.

The cost of air travel has already made it increasingly necessary for people to be able to work "virtually" with colleagues in different places and time zones. Meanwhile, the cost of conducting meetings by teleconference and video conference has dropped significantly. Also, computer software to support asynchronous collaboration—in which individuals don't participate simultaneously, but rather at a time of their own choosing—has become increasingly available. It is also now possible for you and me (or any number of people) to view my computer screen over the Internet and for me to pass control to you so that you can remotely add information to my spreadsheet or correct my document. (My editor and I occasionally used such technology while writing this book.) All of these technologies dramatically improve our ability to collaborate with each other from any place in the world.

**Knowledge Management and Communities of Practice.** Collaborative organizations must be learning organizations. A collaborative organization would use technologies to support the sharing of knowledge and best practices from one part of the organization to another. That way, when employees in one pocket of an organization learned something new, that knowledge could be leveraged throughout the company.

The field of knowledge management has taken off in the last few years, as companies have realized the competitive advantages of capturing and disseminating information about best practices to all of their employees. Virtual communities of practice—networks of employees with similar interests who share information, build community, and learn together regardless of their geographic location or job position—are being encouraged and supported by groupware technology. While technology alone isn't enough to foster learning, it can play an important role in supporting the process of externalizing, documenting, transferring, and applying knowledge throughout an organization.

**E-Learning.** In a collaborative organization, employees would be encouraged to be lifelong learners and to acquire relevant new skills on their own initiative. Consistent with the concept of shared responsibility, individuals can already take more responsibility and control over when and how they learn. It's now possible to access interactive, multimedia learning experiences on one's desktop through the Internet or corporate intranets. This is known as *e-learning*. While training programs delivered over the Web will never replace face-to-face learning entirely, this technology is certainly one of several that collaborative organizations should make use of.

## Reward Systems

Our vision of a collaborative organization includes a new kind of social contract between employers and employees. In return for more meaningful work, access to information, and opportunities for involvement, employees in a collaborative organization would be more proactive, risk taking, and collaborative. The balance sheet of rights and responsibilities might look something like the following.

## Employees' Rights

- Meaningful, mission-driven work

- Appropriate stakeholder involvement

- A safe and healthy workplace

- An equitable economic return

- A workplace in which diversity is valued and promoted

- A socially responsible and ethical organization

- Access to business information

- A culture of integrity, authenticity, and principled relationships

- Open communication

- An opportunity for lifelong learning

## Employees' Responsibilities

- Bring mind as well as body to work

- Work collaboratively and cross-functionally

- Tell the truth as you see it

- Take responsibility for your actions

- Commit to the spirit of the mission

- Actively prepare and participate in collaborative efforts

- Serve your customers with quality

- Commit to lifelong learning and development

Reward and recognition systems in organizations should support and reinforce desired behaviors. Therefore, in a collaborative organization, collaboration and teamwork (as well as support for other core values) would be rewarded, in addition to individual contributions.

Human resource professionals have been struggling for some time with how best to support teamwork. The issues involve what percent of compensation should depend on the performance of the teams on which an individual serves, which teams should be rewarded, how membership on multiple teams should figure into compensation, and what scale of team is most important in determining rewards (e.g., small work teams, profit centers, or the whole company). There are no simple answers to these questions. Perhaps the greatest predictor of a successful reward system is the degree to which employees are involved in designing it. Again, the abstract concept of the collaborative organization and the current reality are beginning to look similar.

## Strategy

In an ideal collaborative organization, as many employees as possible would be involved in developing (or at least reviewing) the core strategies, vision, mission, and long-term objectives of the organization so that they could understand and *own* these elements. Each business unit would convene its own strategic planning meetings. At these meetings, employees would provide input regarding the strategic conversations going on "above" them and integrate overall corporate strategies into their own objectives and strategies. Each employee would thus understand how the corporate mission and strategies applied to his or her tasks. Each person would embody the "corporate DNA," or, as author Meg Wheatley puts it, each person would be seen as a "fractal" of the whole (1999). As a result, groups and individuals would be able to do the right thing without constant direction from above.

Many companies are now involving more employees in strategic planning, rather than depending on consultants. These organizations have discovered that the alignment and education of employees that results from these collaborative discussions about strategy are as important as the planning documents they produce.

## Values

The ideal collaborative organization would be *value driven* in that it would be based on the core values of respect for human dignity, belief in the right of stakeholders to be involved, and commitment to collaborative process. It would also strive to be socially and environmentally responsible. Its mission and values would be openly discussed and presented to the greater community, and would become a source of pride and motivation for its employees. Moreover, its values would offer a kind of competitive advantage in the marketplace and would serve as a means of attracting and retaining a committed workforce.

At Interaction Associates, we have found that both employees and clients are drawn to our organization in part because of our efforts to act in alignment with our values. In general, businesses now seem more willing to talk about values, and many now include statements of values in their strategic plans.

## Skills

Since the skills of collaborative action are so essential to the functioning of a collaborative organization, all employees in such an organization would receive training in facilitative leadership, facilitation, teamwork, coaching, change management, and so forth. This kind of education would give employees a common language of process, thereby enabling people from different parts of the organization to communicate easily with one another about and during collaborative problem-solving processes. The desire for a common language is one of the reasons so many companies are now creating their own training curricula—using a consistent vocabulary helps to build bridges across different business and geographic units.

## Leadership and Culture

As I've mentioned, people with formal decision-making power give "teeth" to a collaborative process. Therefore, a collaborative organization could only exist if its leaders were committed to collaboration and acted congruently with collaborative values. If top management didn't act collaboratively—if they didn't model facilitative leadership—they would communicate the contradictory message, "Do as we say, not as we do." While collaboration can exist in an autocratic bureaucracy, a truly collaborative culture must be supported and promoted from the top of an organization. Therefore, a collaborative organization would have a culture in which people from top to bottom behaved in ways that were congruent with the five principles of collaborative action.

This image of a collaborative organization may seem idealistic and unrealistic to some. Clearly we are all imperfect, so our normal shortcomings are evident in any organization, including a collaborative one. A quick examination of the performance of my own organization over the past thirty years would uncover examples of all of the human failings, from misuse of power to greed to occasional dishonesty. But what is powerful about an organizational culture in which there are built-in checks and balances and sanctions is that inconsistent or deviant behavior is not tolerated. Individuals who don't act consistently with norms and values are confronted from above and below and, as a last resort, are ejected from the system. There have been several dramatic moments at Interaction Associates when employees, even at the partner level, were forced to leave the company because they were so clearly behaving in ways that were not consistent with the collaborative norms that we all espoused. That's what is so powerful about strong cultures.

## Evidence of the High Performance of Collaborative Organizations

So, how do collaborative organizations perform in the marketplace? As I mentioned earlier, few, if any, organizations embody *all* the characteristics of our ideal collaborative organization. And, to date, no specific research has been done to look at the performance of truly collaborative organizations. But much research *has* been done on organizations that exhibit several of the key characteristics—for example, on companies that have strong cultures or are value based. And these studies provide convincing evidence of a strong correlation between these characteristics and outstanding, long-term performance.

For example, John Kotter and James Heskett studied companies that have what they call "adaptive" cultures—cultures that anticipate and adapt to changes in their environment, and in which people actively support each other's efforts to identify problems and implement solutions. In their book *Corporate Culture and Performance* (1992), Kotter and Heskett report that "firms with cultures that emphasized all the key managerial constituencies (customers, stockholders, and employees) and leadership from managers at all levels, outperformed firms that did not have those cultural traits by a huge margin. Over an eleven-year period, the former increased revenues by an average of 682 percent versus 166 percent for the latter, expanded their work forces by 282 percent versus 36 percent, grew their stock prices by 901 percent versus 74 percent, and improved their net incomes by 756 percent versus 1 percent."

In *Built to Last: Successful Habits of Visionary Companies* (1994), James Collins and Jerry Porras describe their research on businesses with outstanding, long-term performance. They found that these companies had strong, "cult-like" cultures built on a small number of core values and a powerful purpose or mission. These visionary companies outperformed the general market by fifteen times and outperformed their comparison companies by six times during the time period from 1926 to 1990.

The study that most relates to collaborative organizations was performed by Professor Daniel Denison at the University of Michigan. Denison tested twelve hundred companies for how well they scored in relation to four cultural traits: mission, involvement, adaptability, and consistency. Dr. Caroline J. Fisher, a student of Denison's work, describes these traits as follows.

**Mission**: The degree to which the company knows why it exists and what its direction is. This is not about your company having a mission that the executive team designed and that is framed nicely on the wall over the copier. It is about shared understanding, alignment, and ownership of that vision throughout your company—with line of sight from job to mission.

**Involvement**: The degree to which individuals at all levels of the company are engaged in and hold that mission as their own. This is not about how involved your managers "say" your front-line workers are. This about how involved your front-line workers say *they* are. And how well people at all levels are positioned, through personal responsibility, authority, accountability, skills, and team orientation, to achieve goals that support the company's mission.

**Adaptability**: The ability of the company to know what customers want, and the degree to which it can respond to external forces and demands. True customer focus is not just about knowing what the customer wants—it is also knowing what you have to learn to provide it, and infusing your organization with that learning.

**Consistency**: The company's systems and processes that support efficiency and effectiveness in reaching goals. This is not about having a nice set of values that are printed on coffee mugs. This is about a defined set of behavioral standards that allow the organization to move beyond restrictive policies and procedures. It is about walking the talk from the top to the front lines. It is about creating a shared language that helps everyone work more smoothly together—thereby increasing speed and efficiency in achieving results. (Fisher and Alford 2000, p. 4)

These four traits do a good job of describing a collaborative culture. Indeed, collaborative action is essential for scoring highly on all four dimensions. And what Denison discovered is that companies with high performance (i.e., an average return on investment [ROI] of 30 percent) scored well on all four traits, as compared to companies with low performance (an average ROI of 9 percent), which scored poorly in these four areas. So, it's reasonable to expect that truly collaborative organizations (by our definition) will, in fact, perform very well in the marketplace.

So, just as thirty years ago what made sense theoretically and what worked in practice converged on the idea of facilitated group problem solving and the Interaction Method, today what makes sense about how organizations should function and what works in practice are converging on the concept of the collaborative organization. After all, it just makes intuitive sense that organizations will function better if people are empowered and supported to work collaboratively on critical issues and opportunities. Collaborative organizations, as we define them, will, by nature be more productive, profitable, adaptive, and socially responsible, and they should have a higher degree of employee satisfaction and loyalty. I have personally experienced the joy of mission-driven and values-based work. I have witnessed my colleagues learning and working enthusiastically and productively in a collaborative culture. So now the question is: How can you build a collaborative culture in your own organization?

## How to Build a Collaborative Organization

The challenge for you as a leader is to lead and support collaboration in your organization from top to bottom. To do this, you must move the key components of a collaborative organization into alignment: organizational structure, information systems, reward systems, strategy, values, skills, and leadership/culture.

It's important that you move the whole system (or a relatively independent subsystem) into alignment at the same time, without allowing any one part to get too far ahead. If, for example, you devote a lot of time and energy to working with your top team and aligning its strategy, culture, rewards, and so forth, but you ignore your middle management, there is bound to be confusion and a decline in morale in the lower parts of the organization. The same is true if you introduce teamwork and collaboration at the bottom or front line of your organization but still reward middle managers for autocratic decision making. Your collaborative culture isn't likely sustain itself. So, at least in theory, you want to introduce innovation and change in parallel at the top, middle, and bottom of your organization.

Part of the reason for this is that when you begin to innovate in one part of a system—to treat it as special—resistance often appears in other parts of the system. This potential conflict is usually most obvious at the boundaries between the new and the old, where people from different cultures are in daily interaction. If some people are being encouraged to cooperate and work cross-functionally while others are still being discouraged from sharing information or working on task forces, there is bound to be confusion and conflict. Often in these boundary conditions, the old culture will dominate the new, because it has the weight of history and familiarity on its side. It's harder to practice new behaviors than to fall back to the old ways of doing things.

So, how can you have collaboration take hold at all levels? It should be no surprise by now that my advice is: Build collaborative organizations collaboratively. The five principles of collaboration in Part II of this book—plus the information in the previous chapter on facilitative leadership—provide most of the guidance you'll need. Let's see how these principles apply to the challenge of systemic change.

### Involve the Relevant Stakeholders

It's essential to build ownership for the change effort in all parts and at all levels of your organization. While the senior management team must be a sponsor of the effort, it can easily get isolated from the rest of the organization and unwittingly become one of the biggest barriers to change. If the effort is driven solely from the top, employees will view it as just another fad or as a desperate action by senior management that will blow over in a few months.

Therefore, it's best to appoint a steering committee to design and manage the effort, one that includes stakeholders from all of the relevant parts and levels of the organization (including senior management). That way, you can create an effective force for change that also serves as a counterbalance to the actions, decisions, and attitudes of top management. The formation of such a steering committee will send a message to the whole organization that the process is open, inclusive, and collaborative. The committee itself can serve as a guardian of the process. If senior leaders continue to act according to old norms, if they continue to exhibit uncollaborative behaviors, the steering committee offers a venue for confronting them. (We've seen this happen many times.) Without a multistakeholder steering committee, the change effort can easily stagnate or get off track.

### Build Consensus Phase by Phase

In the chapter on consensus building, I said that stakeholders must agree on the problem before they can agree on a solution. This principle applies to systems change, as well. Your organization must understand why it needs to change. People must agree on what is not working in the current corporate culture, as well as appreciate what is working. They have to recognize the norms and behaviors that inhibit collaborative action. Employees from all levels must be able to talk openly about the functional and dysfunctional aspects of your organizational culture and acknowledge the ways in which they collude in continuing the old norms. Everyone is part of the system. Everyone bears some responsibility.

In Chapter 7, I gave the example of administrators and physicians who blamed each other for the autocratic culture of their hospital, and then came to acknowledge how both sides colluded in keeping the system the way it was. Administrators and physicians alike felt they could manipulate the system for their own benefit. In another example, the administration of a large private school I worked with wanted to become less paternalistic toward staff and each other and more collaborative in its decision making. The breakthrough occurred when the vice president realized that she treated the president very formally and never confronted him directly when she disagreed with him. She (and he) saw that this behavior communicated to the management team and the rest of the school that openness and directness was neither welcomed nor permitted. Real progress wasn't possible until they acknowledged that their actions sent the wrong message—and then changed their behavior.

Not only does your organization need to agree on what's not working in the current situation, it also needs to agree on a vision of where it's headed. And the vision needs to be linked to the strategy of your organization. In other words, members of the organization need to understand why becoming more collaborative will help the company to be more productive, profitable, competitive, or otherwise successful. They need to understand how collaborative action will help them achieve their mission. If the cultural change isn't seen as a key strategic lever, then it won't be taken seriously or get the attention and resources it needs. If creating a more collaborative work environment doesn't address a significant external issue, such as becoming more competitive or adaptable, responding more effectively to customer needs, or providing higher-quality products, the effort will be viewed as cosmetic and nonessential.

### Design a Process Map
Systemic change takes time. The process of building a truly collaborative organization will take from three to five years, on average. A process map is a very useful tool for designing and managing such a long-term and complex effort. A process map provides a "game board" for laying out the different rings of involvement, phases, and so forth. It forces a group to think about how to balance short-term and long-term issues.

A process map also helps people think through the sequence by which they are going to address the various organizational tracks: culture, strategy, structure, skills, rewards, and technology. My sense is that there's no single right way to sequence the work on these tracks. So much depends on the context. In general, though, strategy needs to be addressed early on in order to get organization-wide agreement on the rationale for the change effort and to figure out how the effort can help the organization achieve its strategic goals.

Addressing the skill track needs to be done fairly early, too, in order to make sure that your organization will have the competencies necessary to support collaborative planning. And cultural change will begin to happen naturally as a by-product of success in dealing with the other tracks collaboratively.

I would caution against working on organizational structure until collaborative skills are widespread in your organization. This is contrary to the conventional approach in which an organization attempts to address challenges simply by restructuring, often because leaders just don't know what else to do. While it's relatively simple to redesign the organization chart, and doing so can make a big splash initially in the organization, you'll be better off in the long run to address issues collaboratively that will have an immediate payoff, such as redesigning a core business process that needs improvement.

Likewise, I wouldn't suggest tackling the more internally focused task of redesigning your reward and recognition systems unless it becomes clear that minor adjustments aren't sufficient and that the compensation system has become a major barrier to progress.

Finally, your organization is probably constantly upgrading its software and hardware. Supporting communications and collaboration should be integrated as one of the design criteria for all future technology enhancements.

The best way to build a collaborative culture is to address issues collaboratively throughout your organization and to transfer collaborative capabilities through just-in-time training. So, the key process design issue is to decide which short-term and long-term issues can be tackled over the next year without overloading your system. Then, the task is to ensure that each track on the game board models effective collaboration, and that it receives the necessary process consulting and training it needs.

## Designate Process Facilitators
## and Harness the Power of Group Memory

Collaborative action always involves numerous meetings, and the quality and productivity of those meetings help to determine the effectiveness of the process. So, from the beginning of a collaborative change process, your meetings need to model the best of collaboration. For example, you should seek to achieve all three dimensions of success in your meetings: results, process, and relationships.

Often there aren't enough well-trained facilitators, recorders, or change management experts within an organization to support a system-wide change effort. Companies often have to depend on external consulting firms to initiate and support these efforts. In order to avoid dependency on such experts and to ensure that collaborative capability is transferred to your organization, however, it's important that you develop a corps of internal process consultants and facilitators as soon as possible. This can best be done by partnering internal and external resources from the beginning, and by transferring responsibility to internal consultants and trainers as their number and competency increases.

## Become a Facilitative Leader

Any successful collaborative change effort requires forceful and effective leadership. To build a collaborative organization, managers must have the will to transform the organization, as well as facilitative leadership skills. The effort doesn't have to depend on one person, however. In fact, the broader the base of support for the change effort and the more that facilitative leadership is diffused through your organization, the more likely the cultural change is to take hold. Ultimately, the culture of your organization won't have shifted until managers from top to bottom are appropriately collaborative in dealing with everyday issues, and until the behaviors of facilitative leadership have become the norm for all managers.

## Conclusion

Like all of the other ideas in this book, the concept of the collaborative organization seems so simple and so intuitively obvious. Trust people, involve them, and give them the skills, tools, and information to work collaboratively. Apply the five principles of collaborative action throughout your organization. Create a mission- and value-driven, supportive work environment. Do all of these things and people will respond and perform beyond your wildest expectations. It makes sense, it's the right thing to do, and it works. Many societal forces are driving organizations in this direction. And yet, the idea of the collaborative organization bucks the stubbornly prevailing wisdom that people need to be "commanded and controlled" and that leaders need to be strong and have the right answers. I'm afraid it will take many years to change conventional notions about how organizations should be designed and led. Nonetheless, in the next chapter I'm going to take yet another leap of imagination and introduce the idea of the collaborative community—which, strangely enough, may be an easier sell.

# Chapter 9

# Collaborative Communities

It's no secret that governance at the community level has grown increasingly difficult in the past half century. Issues have become more complex, stakeholders more numerous and vocal, media scrutiny more intense, and legal battles more common. The level of distrust toward the government has soared.

If you compare our five principles of collaborative action (in Part II) and the concept of facilitative leadership (in Part III) with what goes on daily in civic culture in the United States, it becomes immediately clear why we face governance problems at the community level. The cultural norms of political life violate *all six* powerful ideas about collaborative action. Relevant stakeholders are left out of most planning and decision-making processes. Legislative deliberations jump to solutions before reaching agreement about the nature of the problems, and they operate by majority vote, not consensus. Public planning processes lack clear, open, and understandable process designs. Most public meetings are not facilitated and don't use an effective form of group memory. And elected officials still operate with the belief that they must be solution givers.

Zero for six. No wonder there are breakdowns in community governance.

Despite the daunting nature of the challenges, it seems imperative that we ask: What would happen if we institutionalized collaborative action at the community level? What would happen if leaders in government, as well as in the business and nonprofit sectors, understood and practiced the five principles in this book? What if citizens didn't expect leaders to have all the answers to complex issues facing their community but, instead, were motivated to seek solutions in partnership with their leaders? What would a truly collaborative community look like? And how realistic is this image?

In this chapter, I try to visualize the characteristics of an ideal collaborative community. My vision involves a town or city or county, but it's not hard to extrapolate these ideas to the state or even national level. I will then look at the evidence that these characteristics exist in communities today and the research that points to the benefits of collaboration at the community level. I will end with some suggestions as to what you can do to make your community more collaborative.

## The Characteristics of an Ideal Collaborative Community

So, imagine with me what a collaborative community would look like. First and most important, I believe, the system of leadership and followership would shift to one of partnership. Public leaders would understand that their role is to engage relevant stakeholders in collaborative action, and citizens would expect elected and appointed officials to be facilitative leaders, not to sell simple answers to complex problems. Candidates for public office would be judged and elected on their ability to identify critical issues, engage in dialogue, understand the interactions of complex systems, and communicate the trade-offs clearly, rather than campaign on simple solutions and positions. The social contract between government and its citizens would be similar to that of a contract between a collaborative organization and its employees: the government would provide open, accessible, collaborative decision-making processes in return for a more active, engaged, and informed public. Collaborative action would be the preferred means for addressing all community issues. My friend and colleague David Chrislip provides a good description of the potential benefits of such collaborative action in *The Collaborative Leadership Fieldbook* (2002, p. 18). He writes:

> Collaboration offers a way out of [the current civic] quagmire. It provides a means for crossing the lines drawn by confrontation by bringing all parties together and creating the safety and space for constructive engagement. The possibility of working together embodies the hope for a new kind of politics—a politics of engagement—with a new role for government as a partner with citizens rather than as the primary source of public initiative. Citizens would be the force behind politics instead of its victims. Civic leaders and public officials would take on new leadership roles by bringing citizens together to address common concerns rather than telling them what to do. The skills of consensus-building and collaboration would help build a new civic culture. All of these aspects would lead to a deeper, more constructive, and more inclusive kind of democracy.

Preparation for this kind of civic engagement would begin in the schools. Curricula would focus on process as well as content. Students would become aware of the heuristic nature of human problem solving and would consciously expand their own repertoire of heuristic strategies. Teachers would expect students to learn how to work collaboratively in groups and would build into the curricula modules on group facilitation, teamwork, conflict resolution, and facilitative leadership. The school system as a whole would model effective collaboration—from the deliberations of the school board, to the management style of the superintendent and principals, to the way in which individual schools would engage teachers, parents, and students. Rather than feeling shut out and alienated, students of all ages would help make decisions about issues that directly affected their lives.

A collaborative community would contain numerous collaborative organizations in its business and nonprofit sectors, so adults would also be able to practice and prepare for participation in a collaborative civic culture. Training programs in collaborative skills would be offered within organizations and through open-enrollment programs at local colleges and adult-education centers. The most senior leaders from all sectors would participate in joint leadership programs, which would build trust and understanding among the leaders as well as a common vocabulary and a set of shared concepts about collaborative action.

Consensus-building processes would be under way at all levels of a collaborative community. Neighborhoods would be engaged in collaborative efforts to deal with local issues. Skillful, engaged community residents would shape the decisions that affected their lives. Business and community organizations would engage with city government in public-private partnerships focused on a variety of community-wide issues: housing, education, employment, the arts, public health, and so forth. As part of their commitment to social responsibility, many businesses would form partnerships with low-income groups, through which employees and community members would learn from and support each other. Every few years, the community would engage in a high-involvement process of strategic thinking, through which residents would examine alternative potential futures and create alignment on a common vision of where the community is going, as well as strategic initiatives for getting there.

A variety of technologies would be available for citizens to track the progress of planning and decision-making processes and to participate in a meaningful way. Citizens would have access—through home computers, interactive digital television, and library-based computers—to updated process maps for each planning process, as well as progress reports, group memories of meetings, lists of participants, and times and locations of upcoming meetings. Through these same technologies, citizens could observe and participate in open meetings, contribute their ideas via computer conferences, and register their approval or disapproval of recommendations as they emerge.

To provide the necessary physical and technological support for productive collaborative problem solving, *problem-solving centers* would be built in accessible locations around the community. The largest of these specially designed centers would be located near the city hall and would contain meeting spaces to accommodate small groups of ten to twenty people, as well as large groups of several hundred. Each room would be equipped with computer, audio, and video groupware technology, and staff would be available to provide facilitation, recording, and technical assistance. The central problem-solving center would be linked by high-speed digital connections to a network of smaller centers and meeting rooms located in libraries, schools, and other public spaces throughout the community.

For a few of the most complex and controversial issues facing the community, people would be selected and compensated to sit on citizen panels to gather information, meet with experts, and make recommendations about courses of action. These recommendations would be given great weight in the deliberations of elected officials and sometimes would be submitted directly to the public in the form of referenda.

## Evidence of Collaboration in Communities Today

All the elements of my ideal collaborative community exist somewhere in the United States (or around the world) today. Several communities are well on the way to developing collaborative civic cultures—that is, they embody many of the elements I have described. Clearly, the need for and potential benefits of multiparty collaborative problem solving are becoming widely understood and accepted. Chrislip (2002, p.28) writes:

> Collaborative strategies for addressing public concerns have an importance far beyond that of just another pragmatic tactic for achieving results in the public arena. When these initiatives work, they mitigate conflicts between competing interests, engage citizens deeply in addressing the problems that concern them, and build the capacity to negotiate future conflicts in ways that better reflect the common good. Working together creates the networks, norms, and social trust that facilitate communication and cooperation for mutual benefit. These experiences build bridging social capital rather than destroying it. The continued evolution of the United States as a democratic society depends upon civil society's capacity to foster a new culture of collaborative civic engagement.

In this section, I'll describe some of the evidence that communities are evolving to become more collaborative, and I'll give some specific examples. I'll look first at citizen participation programs and public-private partnerships, and then at dispute resolution efforts, cross-sector leadership development, changes in how school systems operate, corporate responsibility programs, and collaboration technologies.

### Citizen Participation Programs and Public-Private Partnerships

In the 1960s and '70s, the power and impact of the Civil Rights Movement inspired an entire generation to believe that by getting involved they could make a difference. The impulse to collaborate came alive in the form of grassroots action in partnership with the government. Citizen involvement programs such as the Community Action Program and the Community Development Corporations (funded by the federal Model Cities Program) supported the grassroots-driven revitalization of urban areas. Many citywide goal-setting efforts involved thousands of people in setting new directions for their communities.

In the 1980s, the combination of federal disinvestment in communities and social service programs, and the coming of the year 2000, motivated a different kind of collaborative response. Government, business, and community leaders built partnerships to step into the public problem-solving void. Public-private partnerships were created to address issues such as downtown renewal, transportation, education, public health, and the arts. In these partnerships, the private sector made financial contributions, the government sector provided the infrastructure, and the community sector provided volunteers and public support. In an effort to make the best use of dwindling resources, both government and private funders began to require grant seekers to apply as collaboratives and demonstrate how they could reduce duplication and combine resources.

I had the opportunity to assist in the design and facilitation of several of these exciting public-private partnerships. I've mentioned one of them already—the Newark Collaboration Group in Newark, New Jersey, which developed a citywide strategic plan and addressed several critical urban issues. In Denver, Colorado, I assisted in the design and facilitation of a public-private partnership to develop a plan for the future of the downtown area. Over a period of eighteen months, a twenty-eight-person steering committee of government, business, and community leaders (including Mayor Frederico Peña)—supported by a large staff of city planners, two hundred task force members, and hundreds of public meetings—reached consensus on a constitution of values, a planning framework, an access plan, and detailed district plans.

And in Palm Beach County, Florida, my colleagues and I helped design, facilitate, and provide facilitator training for a large consensus-building effort called Project Mosaic, a partnership between the county school district, cities, businesses, and community groups. One of the key agreements reached concerned the linkage between attending a local school and the level of integration in a neighborhood. Participants agreed that if developers built new communities with housing for a diversity of income groups (presumably also drawing a diversity of racial groups), the school system would guarantee that children from those communities could attend their local elementary schools and would not have to be bused outside their neighborhood.

One of the beneficial side effects of collaborative planning processes like these is public awareness of the power of collaborative action. Participants in these processes learn new collaborative skills and apply them naturally in their own organizations.

## Dispute Resolution Programs

The interest in nonadversarial dispute resolution and consensus building has been growing exponentially across the United States In many communities, local organizations offer training in facilitation, mediation, and leadership skills. Many community organizations are seeking to work more collaboratively with their clients and government agencies. In fact, for years nongovernmental organizations (NGOs) around the world have understood that the only way in which they can accomplish their goals of social action is to work collaboratively with other NGOs, donor organizations, and government agencies.

Even the idea of citizen panels has been tested. A *citizen jury* is "a group of randomly selected people, gathered in such a way as to represent a microcosm of their community, who are paid to attend a series of meetings to learn about and discuss a set of candidates in an election or a specific public policy issue and make public recommendations" (Renn, Webler, & Wiedemann, 1995, p. 157). Citizen juries, and similar groups called *planning cells*, have been tested in a number of communities.

## Cross-Sector Leadership Development

The region of Greater Portland, Maine, has made a significant commitment to resolving disputes collaboratively and building a more collaborative civic culture. In 1993, Jim Orr, the president of Unum Life Insurance Company based in Portland, approached the mayor and the president of the chamber of commerce about launching a citywide collaborative effort to explore the idea of a multisector leadership program. These three individuals, in turn, approached me about designing and facilitating this collaborative exploration. The effort resulted in the creation of the Institute for Civic Leadership (ICL), an organization that has graduated six classes of roughly thirty participants each, who were drawn from the highest levels of management in city government, local businesses, and community organizations.

ICL's course, first designed and delivered by David Chrislip and myself, and more recently taught by my colleagues Thomas Rice and Marianne Hughes, meets for a total of fifteen days over six months and includes a three-day Outward Bound trip. During the course, participants are taught facilitative leadership skills and how the principles of collaborative action can be applied in the community and participants' own organizations.

What is so exciting is that there are now almost two hundred graduates who have built strong personal ties with each other and who share a common language about the processes of collaborative action. Periodically, these two hundred influential leaders get together to review the challenges facing their community. They work together to ensure that for each important issue there is a well-designed collaborative effort that involves the appropriate stakeholders and is given adequate resources. The graduates of ICL have become a powerful force for collaborative change in their community. A similar program, the Cascadia Center for Leadership, has been established in Humboldt County, California.

## School Systems

While few school systems explicitly teach problem-solving heuristics, many offer courses in conflict resolution and leadership. School systems have also become much more collaborative in working with teachers and parents. As one example, we at

Interaction Associates have delivered, through local trainers, training courses in facilitative leadership to every *school site committee* in the state of Florida. (A school site committee is a mandated advisory group of administrators, teachers, and parents at every school.) As a result of this training, many of the teachers involved have found ways to be more facilitative in their classrooms. In fact, there is growing evidence to suggest that collaborative schools, like other collaborative organizations, have better student performance than their traditional, authoritarian counterparts.

## Corporate Responsibility Programs

Countless corporations have sought to become good citizens through *corporate community relations* (CCR) programs. Through CCRs, companies give time and money to charities, and encourage their employees to take part in volunteer activities.

Recently, a new model that we call *corporate community exchange* (CCE) has evolved, in which corporations, recognizing their self-interest in the health and well-being of the communities in which they are located, form long-term partnerships with community organizations. Through these partnerships, a two-way exchange of resources and information is established to create social good. Interaction Associates has formed two such partnerships, one in Boston with the Azusa Christian Community, an inner-city community with a focus on outreach to at-risk youth in the Dorchester neighborhood, and one in San Francisco with the Girl's After School Academy in the Sunnydale public housing development. We have received and learned as much as we have given through these programs, and we, as well as our partners, have had our hearts and minds opened on many levels.

## Collaboration Technologies

Much of the technology infrastructure, hardware, and software that I imagined would be set up in an ideal community exists today. Large numbers of citizens can participate in collaborative planning efforts through the use of technologies in all four quadrants of the time/place matrix discussed in Chapter 2. Large numbers of people can gather in one place and interact with one another in small groups, which can be networked together by computers. Individuals can register their responses to questions simultaneously using wireless polling devices. It is possible to "feed forward" information through local TV, radio, and print media, and citizens can give feedback using their telephone, home computers, and TVs connected to cable networks.

All of these support technologies have been used effectively to extend stakeholder involvement in one or more of the countless collaborative planning processes that have been conducted across the United States in the last few years. The groupware technologies exist. Communities just need the political will to fund and use these tools as an ongoing component of their approach to collaborative governance.

## Research on the Benefits of Collaborative Communities

A small but growing body of research documents a link between the level of civic collaboration in a community and the level of public health, access to services, and quality of life. For example, Robert Putnam of the John F. Kennedy School of Government at Harvard University compared the civic cultures of northern and southern Italy. He discovered that towns in northern Italy developed civic cultures with a stronger sense of mutual trust and reciprocity than their feudal and more isolated counterparts in southern Italy—primarily because those in the North had to cooperate with each other to defend themselves against invaders. These differences in civic culture explain why northern Italy has been more successful in dealing with a wide range of modern urban issues, including economic development and public health. Putnam (1993, p. 181) explains:

For at least ten centuries, the North and the South have followed contrasting approaches to the dilemmas of collective action that afflict all societies. In the North, norms of reciprocity and networks of civic engagement have been embodied in tower societies, guilds, mutual aid societies, cooperatives, unions, and even soccer clubs and literary societies. These horizontal civic bonds have undergirded levels of economic and institutional performance generally much higher than in the South, where social and political relations have been vertically structured.... Virtually without exception, the more civic the context, the better the government.... In the civic community, associations proliferate, memberships overlap, and participation spills into multiple arenas of community life. The social contract that sustains such collaboration in the civic community is not legal but moral. The sanction for violating it is not penal, but exclusion from the network of solidarity and cooperation. Norms and expectations play an important role.

Likewise, the National Civic League (NCL) (1998, p. 1) has found evidence for a link between successful, healthy communities and their ability to address issues collaboratively. In *The Civic Index: The National Civic League Model for Improving Community Life*, they write:

The key to success is building—or rebuilding, when necessary—the community's civic infrastructure. In a wide variety of settings—small towns like Sedona, Arizona; the border town of McAleen, Texas; suburban towns like Westminster, Colorado; the old manufacturing center of Lorain, Ohio; the metropolitan areas of Charlotte-Mecklenberg, North Carolina, and Portland, Oregon; and the entire state of New Hampshire—citizens from all sectors and corners of the community have come together to build the community problem-solving capacity. All these communities have looked at the challenges confronting them, considered where they would like to be in the future, agreed on what everyone in the community must do to achieve that vision, and finally, developed an action plan to achieve that vision.

The NCL has developed a Civic Index to help communities evaluate and improve their civic infrastructures. The Civic Index (1998, p. 2) assists communities in developing problem-solving capacity by "providing a method and a process for first identifying and recognizing their strengths and weaknesses, and then structuring collaborative approaches to solving shared problems."

An effort called Healthy Communities/Healthy People, present in fifteen hundred locations around the world, has committed itself to dealing with the "upstream" issues that define and maintain personal and community health. The common conviction is that:

> in healthy communities health-related issues are effectively addressed and a high health status is achieved through broad-based community involvement. Healthy communities focus on the total community—social, economic, geographic, and political—as the ideal context for health promotion. For this reason, private citizens and the business, nonprofit, and governmental sectors must work cooperatively to identify issues and find solutions to them. (Norris & Lampe 1994, p. 6)

Just as for the collaborative organization, all the elements are present in many places for collaborative communities, as I have described them, to emerge and flourish. It will just take a critical mass of people to make it happen. A community must reach the "tipping point," to use the phrase coined by Malcolm Gladwell (2000). Collaborative cultures are developing simultaneously in our organizations as well as in our communities. What works in one context is quickly applied in the other. This cycle of positive reinforcement should continue. The pressing need is for the evolution of collaborative organizations and communities to happen fast enough for society to cope with the complex and critical issues it faces.

## How to Build a Collaborative Community

Clearly, it's possible to change the civic culture of a community, but it takes more time than changing the culture of an organization. The change is more likely to be initiated from the bottom up, by individuals and organizations, than from the top down by elected officials. Elected leaders tend to take the lead from their constituencies rather than the other way around. In any case, the two main cultural change strategies are the same no matter where or how the process is initiated: demonstrate the power of collaboration and transfer the skills to make it possible.

### Demonstrating the Power

For cultural change to take hold, members of a community must experience successful collaborative efforts at every level, from city-wide planning and visioning, to neighborhood consensus building, to collaborative problem solving in their own workplaces. The more that citizens personally experience the power and effectiveness of multistakeholder collaboration, the more they will come to accept this approach and expect it to be the norm, the preferred way of dealing with complex issues. Citizens will come to expect public leaders to initiate and actively participate in open, collaborative processes rather than negotiate deals behind closed doors.

I've found that leaders of organizations often need to test the effectiveness of facilitated collaborative problem solving internally before they will openly advocate for it as a way to resolve public disputes. In 1974, Interaction Associates was approached by the federal Bureau of Land Management (BLM) in California to advise how facilitated, collaborative problem solving could help different interests reach consensus on one of the largest land-use plans ever attempted, the California Desert Plan. At the time, no one believed it was possible to get stakeholders with such strongly held positions to collaborate. Senior managers at the BLM were not willing to try this approach until they had seen it in action behind closed doors. At the time, the BLM had set up a large project office in southern California to draft the plan. The staff was organized around different components of the plan, mirroring the interests of the public: environmental preservation, recreation, agriculture, mining, etc.

So, we went in and facilitated a series of meetings among the staff to help them find common ground on a potential process design for a collaborative effort. During this process, BLM leaders saw how collaborative problem solving worked, and they decided to propose a facilitated planning process involving public interest groups. Like the BLM, businesses and nonprofit organizations often need to test consensus building internally before they can energetically support and know how to participate constructively in facilitated, intersector collaborations. The BLM's effort, one of the first large-scale processes of facilitated collaborative problem solving, resulted in a comprehensive land management plan that garnered broad approval and avoided the major legal challenges so often associated with this kind of plan.

For a community to build a collaborative culture, its government must also begin to operate collaboratively. The mayor and his or her department heads must model the behaviors of facilitative leadership and be comfortable opening up their decision-making processes to internal and external stakeholders. To state the obvious: If local government and many for-profit and nonprofit organizations develop collaborative cultures and have positive experiences collaborating with each other, the community will be well on its way to developing a collaborative culture. It would be a relatively small step for elected officials to declare openly that they are committed to building and maintaining a spirit of collaboration throughout the whole community.

### Transferring the Skills

Systems change because the people in them change. If a significant number of people in a system, even one as large as a town or city, consciously adopt the values and practice the skills of collaborative action in their personal, civic, and work lives, the culture of the whole system will change. So the second approach to systemic change, which should be applied simultaneously with demonstrating the power of collaboration, involves training providing as many opportunities as possible for citizens to be exposed to effective collaborative problem solving and learn the skills of collaborative action.

As I discussed earlier, the leadership program of the Institute for Civic Leadership is effective because leaders from all sectors are learning new skills together, applying these skills within their own organizations as well as in public planning processes, developing strong personal ties of trust and mutual respect, and explicitly discussing the culture of their community and how to support it in becoming more collaborative. The graduates of such programs have a common language and a shared set of values, and collectively become a powerful force for change.

My colleagues at the Interaction Institute for Social Change provide another illustration of the fact that it is possible to launch a community on the pathway of cultural change. They have been engaged in helping to build a civil society in Northern Ireland. In partnership with the Workers' Educational Association there, the IISC has trained more than five hundred local leaders in facilitative leadership skills. These leaders are now applying the skills in their own work. The IISC has also trained seventeen trainers/facilitators who are continuing to transfer the skills and tools necessary for cross-sectarian community and economic development to the grassroots leaders who must deliver on the promise of peace and social justice in Northern Ireland.

## Conclusion

Over the past thirty years, communities' acceptance of multistakeholder collaboration has increased dramatically. In communities in which the idea of facilitation was once unknown, many organizations like Interaction Associates and the IISC now deliver high-quality process consulting and training services. I believe our communities are becoming more collaborative every day. All we have to do is keep pushing on the two prongs of the change effort: demonstrating the power of collaborative action and providing opportunities for people to develop collaborative skills.

Chapter 10

# Where to Go
# from Here

So, how might you begin to make collaboration work in your group, organization, or community? To paraphrase the words of my Eastern European friends (who I introduced in the preface), "If you can grasp these few powerful ideas in your heart, then you will be able to sing." The place to begin, right now, is in your heart. Try to hold in your heart two powerful ideas: (1) every human being has the right to be involved in decisions that affect his or her life, and (2) with good process, people can generate more creative and comprehensive solutions collaboratively than they can by themselves. Trust and believe in these two fundamental ideas, and you will be well on your way to making music. Mastery of the tools and techniques of collaboration will follow.

I have learned to sing the song of collaboration by trusting the process, and then by just diving in. From my first conscious steps to build a collaborative organization in 1969, I have been blessed by the lifelong journey of learning and growth that has followed. So, my second piece of advice is: Dive in. Experiment. Try new behaviors. Share with your colleagues a few of the simple but powerful ideas you've learned from this book, and test them out. Thanks to the checks and balances of facilitated, collaborative problem solving, you will all learn together. If you are sincere in your commitment to being collaborative and inclusive, others will be tolerant when you stumble. If you model openness and a desire to learn, you will help everyone learn to collaborate together.

I suggest that you start with a relatively easy issue in a familiar place—with your most immediate group or team. Here are some ideas for first steps you could take.

### As a leader

- Try using a decision-making option with a higher level of involvement. For example, rather than gathering input from individuals and then making a decision, try gathering input from the whole team and then deciding. (See Fig. 19 on page 181.)

- Ask someone else to facilitate an important meeting.

- Stay in problem space and vision space before jumping to solutions.

- Create a process map for your next meeting or planning process.

- Try to be collaborative and make your words and actions congruent. For example, use "we" rather than "I."

### As a participant

- Use facilitative interventions in your next meeting, such as getting group members to agree on a common process before they start talking about substantive issues.

- Identify other relevant stakeholders and suggest that they be included in your next important meeting.

- Encourage your group to work for consensus before resorting to win-lose decision-making processes.

- Try rearranging the chairs in a semicircle for your next meeting, and offer to record ideas on chart pad paper.

The first time you trust the process of collaboration, it can be a little frightening. You may feel a little out of control. It's like a "trust fall"—a team-building exercise in which you allow yourself to fall straight backwards into the hands of your team members. That's exactly how I have felt a number of times when the only way to move forward was to trust the process of collaborative action and the good intentions of my colleagues—trust that we could and must resolve the issue collaboratively. At one point in the late '70s, for example, a number of principals had left Interaction Associates for a variety of reasons, and I wasn't sure there were enough of us left to continue the business. The only way to know was to open the issue up to the whole organization and see what would happen. I remember defining the issue as: Are we on the same mountain, and do we want to climb it together?

To address this issue, we hired an external facilitator and met for a day in our conference room in San Francisco. Everyone had an opportunity to express in words and pictures how he or she saw the mountain we faced—our mission. After several hours of listening to each other and working together, we were able to describe an image of where we headed—an image that was understood and agreed upon by all. The final process was so memorable and moving. One by one, the facilitator asked us, "Are you on this mountain, and are you committed to climbing it together?" One by one each person stood up and made that commitment. We had rebuilt a foundation of agreements that allowed us to move forward. And I regained confidence in our ability to succeed together. The process of collaboration had worked.

And it can work for you too. If you'd like to learn more about collaboration as you begin to test it out, there are several things you might do, depending on your style of learning. If you learn best through the printed page, you might start by rereading this book and taking some notes. Then you might read one or more of the excellent books listed in the Resources section. As I'm sure you know, if you read only one book on a subject, then you are trapped by the point of view of that author (in this case, me). If you read several books, you will be forced to draw your own conclusions.

The same is true if you are an experiential learner. I'd suggest you take at least two or more of the countless courses that are offered on such topics as group facilitation, leadership, teamwork, and change management. Or better yet, contract with someone to come in and train your whole group. You could also hire a facilitator to help your team work through some real-world problem. Or, participate in some other collaborative effort in your organization or in your community. You can learn a lot from just observing a well-facilitated collaborative process.

With learning and practice, you can make collaboration work for you. It's effective, it's energizing, and it is the right thing to do. As I have asserted in the last two chapters, I believe that the power of collaborative action holds great promise for our organizations and communities as a means of building more humane and productive places to work and live. Collaboration offers a way for our democratic societies to move beyond the win-lose mechanisms of majority voting to develop more inclusive, win-win ways of solving problems and making decisions. It is really a question of individual and collective will. Do we want to be collaborative? I hope and trust that we do.

# Resources

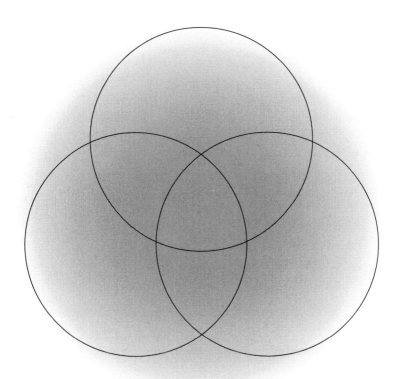

# Bibliography

Adams, James L. 1974. *Conceptual Blockbusting*. San Francisco: W. H. Freeman.

Adams, John D., ed. 1998. *Transforming Leadership*. 2nd ed. Alexandria, Va: Miles River Press.

Albert, Burt. 1996. *Fat Free Meetings: How to Make Them Fast, Focused and Fun!* Princeton, N.J.: Peterson's.

Argyris, Chris. 1993. *Knowledge for Action: A Guide to Overcoming Barriers to Organizational Change*. San Francisco: Jossey-Bass.

———. 1993. *Organizational Learning II: Theory, Method, and Practice*. San Francisco: Jossey-Bass.

Axelrod, Robert. 1984. *The Evolution of Cooperation*. New York: Basic Books.

Bardach, Eugene. 1998. *Getting Agencies to Work Together: The Practice and Theory of Managerial Craftsmanship*. Washington, D.C.: The Brookings Institution Press.

Beckhard, Richard. 1997. *Agent of Change: My Life, My Practice*. San Francisco: Jossey-Bass.

Beckhard, Richard, and Reuben T. Harris. 1987. *Organizational Transitions: Managing Complex Change*. Reading, Mass.: Addison-Wesley.

Beckhard, Richard, and Wendy Pritchard. 1992. *Changing the Essence: The Art of Creating and Leading Fundamental Change in Organizations*. San Francisco: Jossey-Bass.

Bennis, Warren. 1989. *On Becoming a Leader*. Reading, Mass.: Addison-Wesley.

———. 1989. *Why Leaders Can't Lead: The Unconscious Conspiracy Continues*. San Francisco: Jossey-Bass.

Bennis, Warren, Kenneth D. Benne, and Robert Chin, eds. 1985. *The Planning of Change*. New York: Holt, Reinhart & Winston.

Bennis, Warren, and Patricia Ward Biederman. 1997. *Organizing Genius: The Secrets of Creative Collaboration*. Reading, Mass.: Addison-Wesley.

Bennis, Warren, and Bert Nanus. 1985. *Leaders: The Strategies for Taking Charge.* New York: Harper & Row.

Block, Peter. 1999. *Flawless Consulting: A Guide to Getting Your Expertise Used.* San Francisco: Jossey-Bass/Pfeiffer.

———. 1993. *Stewardship: Choosing Service Over Self-Interest.* San Francisco: Berrett-Koehler.

———. 1987. *The Empowered Manager: Positive Political Skills at Work.* San Francisco: Jossey-Bass.

Bois, J. Samuel. 1966. *The Art of Awareness.* Dubuque, Iowa: W. C. Brown.

Bradford, Leland. 1976. *Making Meetings Work: A Guide for Leaders and Group Members.* La Jolla, Calif.: Leland Bradford University Associates.

Bridges, William. 1991. *Managing Transitions: Making the Most of Change.* Reading, Mass,: Addison-Wesley.

Buckingham, Marcus, and Curt Coffman. 1999. *First, Break All the Rules: What the World's Greatest Managers Do Differently.* New York: Simon & Schuster.

Cartwright, Dorwin, and Alvin Zander, 1968. *Group Dynamics,* 3rd Ed. New York: Harper & Row.

Chrislip, David D. 2002. *Collaborative Leadership Fieldbook.* San Francisco: Jossey-Bass.

Chrislip, David D., and Carl E. Larson. 1994. *Collaborative Leadership: How Citizens and Civic Leaders Can Make a Difference.* San Francisco: Jossey-Bass.

Collins, James C., and Jerry I. Porras. 1994. *Built to Last: Successful Habits of Visionary Companies.* New York: Harper Business.

Covey, Stephen R. 1989. *The Seven Habits of Highly Effective People.* New York: Simon & Schuster.

Daniels, William. 1986. *Group Power I: A Manager's Guide to Regular Meetings.* San Diego: University Associates.

———. 1990. *Group Power II: A Manager's Guide to Regular Meetings.* San Diego: University Associates.

Diebold, John. 1984. *Making the Future Work: Unleashing the Power of Innovation for the Decade Ahead.* New York: Simon & Schuster.

Dixon, Nancy. 1994. *The Organizational Learning Cycle.* New York: McGraw-Hill.

Doyle, Michael, and David Straus. 1976 *How to Make Meetings Work.* New York: Jove Books.

Eddy, William B., et al. 1969. *Behavioral Science and The Manager's Role.* Washington, D.C.: NTL Learning Resources Corp.

Eden, Collin, and Chris Huxham. 2001. The negotiation of purpose in multi-organizational collaborative groups. *Journal of Management Studies* 38, no. 3: 374-391.

Fisher, Caroline J. 2000. Like it or not, culture matters: Linking culture to bottom line business performance. *Employee Relations Today* 27: 46-49.

Fisher, Caroline J. and R. J. Alford, 2000. Consulting on culture: A new bottom line. *Consulting Psychology Journal* 52: 3–4.

Fisher, Roger, and William Ury. 1991. *Getting To Yes.* New York: Penguin Books.

Fox, Matthew. 1994 *The Reinvention of Work: A New Vision of Livelihood for Our Time.* San Francisco: HarperSanFrancisco.

Frank, Milo O. 1989. *How to Run a Successful Meeting in Half the Time.* New York: Simon & Schuster.

Fukuyama, Francis. 1995. *Trust: The Social Virtues and the Creation of Prosperity.* New York: The Free Press.

Gawain, Shakti. 1982. *Creative Visualization.* New York: Bantam New Age.

Gelinas, Mary V., and Roger G. James. 1998. *Collaborative Change: Improving Organizational Performance.* San Francisco: Jossey-Bass/Pfeiffer.

Gery, Gloria. 1991. *Electronic Performance Support Systems.* Boston: Weingarten.

Gladwell, Malcolm. 2000. *The Tipping Point: How Little Things Can Make a Big Difference.* Boston: Little, Brown.

Hall, Lavinia, ed. 1993. *Negotiation: Strategies for Mutual Gain.* Thousand Oaks, Calif.: Sage.

Hamel, Gary, and C. K. Prahalad. 1994. *Competing for the Future.* Boston: Harvard Business School Press.

Heckscher, Charles. 1996. Can business beat bureaucracy? *The American Prospect* 5: 114-128.

Heckscher, Charles, and Anne Donnellon, eds. 1994. *The Post-Bureaucratic Organization: New Perspectives on Organizational Change.* Newbury Park, Calif.: Sage.

Heifetz, Ronald A. 1994. *Leadership Without Easy Answers.* Cambridge: Belknap Press.

Herbert, Theodore T., and Edward B. Yost. 1979. A comparison of decision quality under normal and interacting consensus group formats: The case of the structured problem. *Decision Sciences* 10, no. 3: 358-71.

Howard, V. A., and J. H. Barton. 1992. *Thinking Together: Making Meetings Work.* New York: William Morrow & Company.

Howell, Johnna L. 1995. *Tools for Facilitating Team Meetings.* Seattle: Integrity Publishing.

Huxham, Chris, and Siv Vangen. 2000. Ambiguity, complexity, and dynamics in the membership of collaboration. *Human Relations* 53, no. 6: 771-806.

———. 2000. Leadership in the shaping and implementation of collaboration agendas: How things happen in a (not quite) joined-up world." *Academy of Management Journal* 43, no. 6: 1159-1175.

———. 2000. Nurturing collaborative relations: Building trust in interorganizational collaboration. The University of Strathclyde, Graduate School of Business. Working Paper no. 2000-014R.

———. 2000. "What Makes Partnerships Work." In *Public-Private Partnerships,* edited by Stephen P. Osborne 293-309. New York: Routledge.

Johansen, Robert, and Rob Swigart. 1994. *Upsizing the Individual in the Downsized Organization.* Reading, Mass.: Addison-Wesley.

Kaner, Sam, et al. 1996. *Facilitator's Guide to Participatory Decision-Making.* Philadelphia: New Society.

Kanter, Rosabeth M. 1985. *The Change Masters: Innovations for Productivity in the American Corporation.* New York: Simon & Schuster.

Kepner, Charles H., and Benjamin B. Tregoe. 1965. *The Rational Manager.* New York: McGraw-Hill.

Kieffer, George D. 1988. *The Strategy of Meetings.* New York: Warner Books.

Kilmann, Ralph H. 1987. *Beyond the Quick Fix: Managing Five Tracks to Organizational Success.* San Francisco: Jossey-Bass.

Kleiner, Art. 1996. *The Age of Heretics.* New York: Doubleday.

Kotter, John P. 1990. *A Force for Change: How Leadership Differs from Management.* New York: Free Press.

Kotter, John P., and James L. Heskett. 1992. *Corporate Culture and Performance.* New York: Free Press.

Kouzes, James M., and Barry Z. Posner. 1993. *Credibility: How Leaders Gain and Lose It, Why People Demand It.* San Francisco: Jossey-Bass.

————. 1995. *The Leadership Challenge: How to Keep Getting Extraordinary Things Done in Organizations.* San Francisco: Jossey-Bass Publishers.

Kraus, William A. 1980. *Collaboration in Organizations: Alternatives to Hierarchy.* New York: Kluwer Academic.

Lipnack, Jessica, and Jeffrey Stamps. 1994. *The Age of the Network: Organizing Principles for the 21st Century.* New York: John Wiley & Sons.

————. 1993. *The TeamNet Factor: Bringing the Power of Boundary Crossing into the Heart of Your Business.* Essex Junction, Vt.: Oliver Wight Publishers.

————. 2000. *Virtual Teams: People Working Across Boundaries With Technology.* New York: John Wiley & Sons.

Lippitt, Gordon, Petter Langseth, and Jack Mossop. 1985. *Implementing Organizational Change.* San Francisco: Jossey-Bass.

Lippitt, Gordon, and Ronald Lippitt. 1986. *The Consulting Process in Action.* San Diego: University Associates.

McCaffrey, David, Sue Faerman, and David Hart. 1995. The appeal and difficulties of participative systems. *Organization Science* 6, no. 6: 603-27.

McKim, Robert H. 1972. *Experiences in Visual Thinking.* Monterey, Calif.: Brooks/Cole Publishing.

McPherson, Joseph H. 1967. *The People, the Problems, and the Problem-Solving Methods.* Midland, Mich.: The Pendell Company.

Michaelsen, Larry K., Warren E. Watson, and Robert H. Black. 1989. A realistic test of individual versus group consensus decision making. *Journal of Applied Psychology* 74, no. 5: 834-840.

Mohrman, Allan M., Jr., et al. 1989. *Large-Scale Organizational Change.* San Francisco: Jossey-Bass.

Nanus, Burt. 1992. *Visionary Leadership: Creating a Compelling Sense of Direction for Your Organization.* San Francisco: Jossey-Bass.

National Civic League. 1998. *The Civic Index: The National Civic League Model for Improving Community Life.* Denver, Colo.: National Civic League.

Neisser, Ulrich. 1967. *Cognitive Psychology*. New York: Appleton-Century-Crofts.

Newell, Allen, and Herbert A. Simon. 1972. *Human Problem Solving*. Englewood Cliffs, N.J.: Prentice-Hall.

Norris, Tyler, and David Lampe. 1994. Healthy communities, healthy people." *National Civic Review*, Summer-Fall.

O'Hara-Devereaux, Mary, and Robert Johansen. 1994. *GlobalWork*. San Francisco: Jossey-Bass.

Ostroff, Frank. 1999. *The Horizontal Organization: What the Organization of the Future Looks Like and How it Delivers Value to Customers*. New York: Oxford University Press.

Presley, J., and Keen, S. 1975. Better meetings lead to higher productivity: A case study. *Management Review*, April.

Prince, George M. 1970. *The Practice of Creativity: A Manual for Dynamic Group Problem Solving*. New York: Harper & Row.

Putnam, Robert D. 1993. *Making Democracy Work: Civic Traditions in Modern Italy*. Princeton, N.J.: Princeton University Press.

Rayner, Steven R. 1993. *Recreating the Workplace: The Pathway to High Performance Work Systems*. Essex Junction, Vt.: Oliver Wight Publications.

Renn, Ortwin, Thomas Webler, and Peter Wiedemann. 1995. *Fairness and Competence in Citizen Participation: Evaluating Models for Environmental Discourse*. Boston: Kluwer Academic.

Rogers, Carl R. 1969. *Freedom to Learn*. Columbus, Ohio: C. E. Merrill Publishing.

Rosen, Robert H. 1996. *Leading People: Transforming Business from the Inside Out*. New York: Viking.

Schaef, Anne Wilson, and Diane Fassel. 1988. *The Addictive Organization*. San Francisco: Harper & Row.

Schein, Edgar H. 1985. *Organizational Culture and Leadership*. San Francisco: Jossey-Bass.

————. 1969. *Process Consultation: Its Role in Organization Development*. Reading, Mass.: Addison-Wesley.

Schindler-Rainman, Eva. 1988. *Taking Your Meetings Out of the Doldrums*. San Diego: University Associates.

Schutz, Will. 1994. *The Human Element: Productivity, Self-Esteem and the Bottom Line*. San Francisco: Jossey-Bass.

Schwarz, Roger M. 1994. *The Skilled Facilitator: Practical Wisdom for Developing Effective Groups.* San Francisco: Jossey-Bass.

Senge, Peter M. 1994. *The Fifth Discipline Fieldbook: Strategies and Tools for Building a Learning Organization.* New York: Currency Doubleday.

—————. 1990. *The Fifth Discipline: The Art and Practice of the Learning Organization.* New York: Currency Doubleday.

Spencer, Laura J. 1989. *Winning Through Participation: Meeting the Challenge of Corporate Change with the Technology of Participation.* Dubuque, Iowa: Kendall/Hunt Publishing.

Susskind, Lawrence, Sarah McKearnan, and Jennifer Thomas-Larmer, eds. 1999. *The Consensus Building Handbook: A Comprehensive Guide to Reaching Agreement.* Thousand Oaks, Calif.: Sage.

Thomas, Gordon. 1980. *Leader Effectiveness Training.* New York: Bantam Books.

Tichy, Noel. 1983. *Managing Strategic Change: Technical, Political and Cultural Dynamics.* New York: John Wiley & Sons.

Toffler, Alvin. 1985. *The Adaptive Corporation.* New York: McGraw Hill.

Ulschak, Francis, Leslie Nathanson, and Peter Gillan. 1981. *Small Group Problem Solving: An Aid to Organizational Effectiveness.* Reading, Mass.: Addison-Wesley.

Weisbord, Marvin R. 1987. *Productive Workplaces: Organizing and Managing for Dignity, Meaning, and Community.* San Francisco: Jossey-Bass.

Wheatley, Margaret J. 1999. *Leadership and the New Science: Discovering Order in a Chaotic World.* San Francisco: Berrett-Koehler.

Wickelgren, Wayne A. 1938. *How to Solve Problems: Elements of a Theory of Problems and Problem Solving.* San Francisco: W. H. Freeman.

# Additional Models

This section includes five models referenced in the text: the 64 Heuristics, the Stages of Discussion model, the Expanded Interaction Method, the complete Facilitative Leadership model, and the Chartering Checklist. The descriptions of these models are very brief. For further information and explanation, please contact Interaction Associates or the Interaction Institute for Social Change.

## The 64 Heuristics

From 1969 to 1973, with the support of the Carnegie Corporation of New York, my colleagues and I identified the following list of 64 heuristic strategies. We organized the heuristics into categories and, in a self-published pamphlet called the *Strategy Notebook*, presented them mainly in terms of pairs of opposing, transitive verbs. Using this list as a foundation, we developed and taught a course and a teacher-training program in problem solving called Tools for Change. Our efforts to identify these heuristics were not scientific or rigorous, but the resulting list served us well in our training programs.

Each heuristic is a discrete strategy for approaching a problem, and each has a specific set of powers and limitations. Also, these heuristic "atoms" can be combined in various ways to make up a huge number of more complex problem-solving "molecules."

### Metaheuristics

Change
Vary
Cycle
Repeat

## Master Heuristics

Build Up/Eliminate

Work Forwards/Work
Backwards

## Strategies for Set Manipulation

Associate/Classify

Generalize/Exemplify

Compare/Relate

## Strategies for Involvement

Commit/Defer

Leap In/Hold Back

Focus/Release

Force/Relax

Dream/Imagine

Purge/Incubate

## Strategies for Manipulating Information

Display/Organize

List/Check

Diagram/Chart

Verbalize/Visualize

## Strategies for Information Retrieval

Memorize/Recall

Record/Retrieve

Search/Select

## Strategies for Dealing with the Future

Plan/Predict

Assume/Question

Hypothesize/Guess

Define/Symbolize

Simulate/Test

## Strategies for Physical Manipulation

Play/Manipulate

Copy/Interpret

Transform/Translate

Expand/Reduce

Exaggerate/Understate

Adapt/Substitute

Combine/Separate

## The Stages of Discussion Model

To help people to get started facilitating meetings, we have found that it helps to present the last three phases of problem solving (i.e., generating alternatives, evaluating, and decision making) in terms of the following "Open-Narrow-Close" model (fig. 20).

1. **Open:** People offer ideas, opinions, or information.

2. **Narrow:** The information is organized for better understanding and/or is evaluated.

3. **Close:** Specific proposals are refined and agreements are made; other information is set aside for future discussion.

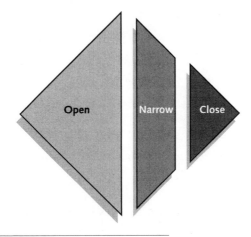

**Figure 20:** Stages of discussion

## The Expanded Interaction Method

In our courses, we have expanded the concept of the Interaction Method to include more than simply the four self-correcting meeting roles and responsibilities (facilitator, recorder, manager/chairperson, participant). We now see the Interaction Method as *a*

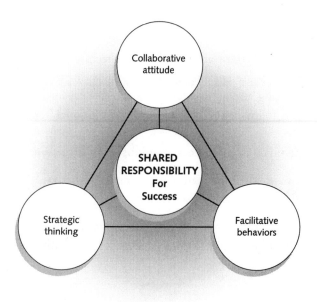

**Figure 21:** The Interaction Method

*collaborative approach for building understanding and agreements among people.* (See fig. 21.)

- **Shared responsibility** is the *principle* that everyone in a meeting can play an active and positive role in producing meaningful results.

- **Collaborative attitude** is the *mindset* that guides individuals to act in a cooperative and effective manner.

- **Strategic thinking** is the *mental process* of selecting an appropriate course of action to achieve desired results.

- **Facilitative behaviors** are the *practical tools, techniques, and actions* that help people build understanding and agreement.

## The Complete Facilitative Leadership Model

Interaction Associates uses the following model of facilitative leadership in its courses (fig. 22). It describes the facilitative leader in terms of seven practices (described below). In this book, I focused on the role of the leader *in supporting collaborative action,* which involves three main practices: seek maximum appropriate involvement, design pathways to action, and facilitate agreement.

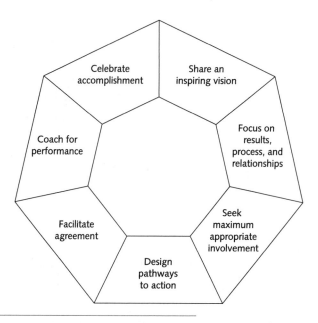

**Figure 22:** Seven Practices of the Facilitative Leader

**Share an Inspiring Vision.** Facilitative leaders create and communicate an inspiring image of the future, and enroll others in its pursuit. People work with greater commitment when they are guided by a vision and believe their efforts can make a difference. However, the pressures of daily work often distract people, narrowing their focus and restricting their view of what is possible. By sharing their vision and values, leaders keep the mission out front, like a beacon, guiding people toward greater achievement.

**Focus on Results, Process, and Relationship.** Facilitative leaders build a framework for performance and satisfaction by balancing their focus among results, process, and relationship. While monitoring bottom-line performance (results), leaders also encourage continuous improvement in the way the work gets done (process), and how people treat each other in the workplace (relationship). Balancing these three dimensions of success enables leaders to produce results, sustain productivity and quality, and build a supportive work environment.

**Seek Maximum Appropriate Involvement.** People want to participate in decisions that affect their daily work lives. Facilitative leaders make conscious choices about when and how people can best participate. They leverage the interest and talent of those around them by including them appropriately in decision-making processes. Seeking maximum appropriate involvement pays several dividends—better communication, more informed decisions, increased commitment to action, and higher levels of trust.

**Design Pathways to Action.** Good planning increases the likelihood of successful implementation. Facilitative leaders guide others in planning how to solve problems and realize opportunities. They help people see alternative paths to the desired result and suggest ways to evaluate which routes are best. By providing a map of the road ahead, leaders build confidence that the goal is attainable and increase the likelihood of successful implementation.

**Facilitate Agreement.** People notice what leaders say and do, taking their cues from the leader's behavior. Facilitative leaders model behaviors that create a safe environment for participation and teamwork. They encourage diversity of opinion and honor individual perspectives, while helping team members stay focused on the task at hand. By facilitating understanding and agreement, leaders demonstrate the power of teamwork to produce clear decisions and quality results.

**Coach for Performance.** Facilitative leaders coach individuals to do their best. They encourage people to think outside the norm, to experiment and take risks, and to overcome habits that restrict thinking. The leader's most valuable tool is the ability to listen as an ally, to consciously support the expression of others' ideas and aspirations. By working as supportive coaches, facilitative leaders build environments in which people learn and grow.

**Celebrate Accomplishment.** Dozens of opportunities for thanking people emerge over the course of a work week. Facilitative leaders seize these moments to celebrate small successes and acknowledge individuals and teams for their contributions. People are invigorated by authentic acknowledgment and celebration. By taking time out to recognize performance, facilitative leaders build pride, self-esteem, and a sense of commitment to the group or organization.

## Chartering Checklist

This checklist identifies the key tasks in the chartering process that help set up a team for success. Use this list to monitor the progress and completion of the chartering process.

| Done | Attribute | Notes/Steps to complete |
|:---:|---|---|
| | **Shared and Meaningful Purpose** *The team's task or reason for existing that is shared by all team members and, in some way, motivates and inspires each.* | |
| ☐ | Define the reason for calling the team together by identifying the opportunity or problem the team is addressing. | |
| ☐ | Identify, in general terms, why this work is meaningful/important to the organization, customer and/or members of the team. | |
| ☐ | Describe what success would look like if the team accomplished its purpose. | |
| | **Specific and Challenging Goals** *The measurable results the team agrees to produce that will satisfy an important organizational need and demand extraordinary performance by the team leader and members.* | |
| ☐ | Define needs/expectations of the organization, internal key stakeholders and external customers that the team is required to meet. | |
| ☐ | Translate expectations into measurable performance goals that: • are challenging enough to the team to keep them motivated, yet are still attainable. | |

| Done | Attribute | Notes/Steps to complete |
|:---:|:---|:---|
| | • are unambiguous in their description so that it is clear if and by when the goals have been accomplished. <br>• include the performance indicators by which the results will be assessed and completion dates. <br>• reference team success in terms of results, process and relationship satisfaction. | |
| ☐ | Identify clear priorities when competing goals exist. | |
| ☐ | Define any boundaries or constraints governing the team's work (i.e., the scope of the project). | |
| ☐ | Identify the resources the team will require in order to meet its goals (budget, materials, equipment, information, training, additional personnel) and make agreements with the team about their acquisition. | |
| | **Clear Roles** <br>*A shared understanding by team sponsor, leader, and members of how the responsibilities for specific team functions and tasks will be distributed.* | |
| ☐ | Clarify with team leader and members who will take responsibility for the key process functions of: <br>• team facilitation/meeting management. <br>• information management. <br>• decision making. <br>• stakeholder management and communication. <br>• team performance management. | |
| ☐ | Ensure that the team is clear about the level of involvement being used for each major decision. | |

| Done | Attribute | Notes/Steps to complete |
|:---:|:---|:---|
| ☐ | Communicate the chosen levels of involvement in decision making. | |
| | **Common and Collaborative Approach** *Commonly understood plans and methods for accomplishing tasks in ways that facilitate participation, cooperation, and mutual support.* | |
| ☐ | Ensure that team operating agreements and principles are built concerning:<br>• when and how often the team needs to meet.<br>• norms or ground rules for which the team wishes to hold each other accountable.<br>• liaison to the sponsor and other key stakeholders. | |
| ☐ | Ensure that a complete preliminary work plan is developed including:<br>• major phases or segments of the project.<br>• major milestones the team will achieve and by when.<br>• task assignments.<br>• action plans.<br>• review plans. | |
| ☐ | Identify and discuss any key issues or anticipated barriers to the team's success. | |

| Done | Attribute | Notes/Steps to complete |
|------|-----------|-------------------------|
| | **Complementary Skills and Resources** *The appropriate combination of knowledge, ability, and experience required for the team to perform effectively along with the necessary means to do the work.* | |
| ☐ | Identify the mix of skills and experience necessary for the team's success: <br> • functional/task-related competence. <br> • collaborative process competence. <br> • interpersonal management competence. | |
| ☐ | Identify who on the team can fulfill these skill requirements (and, if not present on the team, how the skills will be accommodated or developed). | |

# About Interaction Associates

Interaction Associates, Inc., builds organizational capability to achieve strategic objectives by maximizing executive, team, and individual performance. Our services include change management consulting, organizational development consulting, and the design and delivery of leadership development programs and learning systems.

### Change Management and Organizational Consulting

We help our clients maintain performance and retain top talent during periods of major change by aligning their strategies with their management systems. Working across multiple levels and functions, we translate strategies into action plans with clear accountabilities, deliverables, and timelines.

### Leadership Development and Learning Systems

Interaction Associates provides more than a roadmap for organizational development and transformation. We develop more effective leaders, teams, coaches, and internal consultants. We draw upon years of experience with strategic thinking, collaboration, team building, group facilitation, instructional design, and experiential learning (both online and classroom) to create management and leadership development programs for some of the best-run companies in America and the world. Since its founding, Interaction Associates has consulted and provided training services to more than one thousand organizational clients. These include 175 of the *Fortune* 500 corporations, government agencies, and nonprofit organizations worldwide.

For further information, please visit our Web site at: *www.interactionassociates.com.*

# About the Interaction Institute for Social Change

In 1993, Interaction Associates created the nonprofit Interaction Institute for Social Change (IISC) and committed 10 percent of IA's pretax profits and up to ten paid days per year of every employee's time to the work of IISC. Since then, the IISC has both drawn on the resources of IA and established itself as a distinctive organization with deep community experience, high-level collaborative skill, and multicultural staff and affiliates who reflect the communities it serves.

To achieve its mission, IISC provides training, coaching, consulting, and facilitation services; facilitates partnerships across sectors; and provides networking opportunities for social change agents. IISC contributes to social change by focusing these services on transforming social- and public-sector organizations, public schools and education systems, and communities. In particular, IISC:

- guides *organizations in the social and public sectors* toward becoming more participatory, just, and high-performing workplaces, and more engaged participants in community change.

- supports *educational leaders* in developing the skills and tools for leading effectively and for promoting collaborative school communities.

- offers *civic leadership development* experiences for grassroots, neighborhood, and organizational leaders who are working to transform their communities from the inside out.

- facilitates *collaborative planning processes and community dialogues* for coalitions that involve many constituencies, as well as for advocacy organizations, and neighborhood groups.

- supports people in nonprofit organizations, corporations, and government agencies to *build partnerships and alliances* that focus on creating a more just society and a fair chance for all.

Since its founding, IISC has worked with small and large nonprofit organizations, volunteer civic associations, coalitions, public agencies, and partnerships that involve corporations and community groups across the United States. Internationally, IISC works with community leaders who are creating new civic institutions and partnerships for peace.

For more information, visit the IISC's Web site at *www.interactioninstitute.org.*

# Index

# About the Author

David Straus founded Interaction Associates in 1969. Over the years, he has served in every major leadership position in the company, including president, CEO, and chairman of the board. Under his guidance, Interaction Associates has become a recognized leader in organizational development, group process facilitation, training, and consulting.

Mr. Straus guided the development of Interaction Associates' consulting practice and training programs. He was also responsible for major change efforts in a variety of organizations, including the health care and service industries. He has worked with social action partnerships in Newark, New Jersey, and Palm Beach County, Florida, as well.

Mr. Straus earned a Bachelor's degree from Harvard University and a Master's degree in architecture from Harvard's Graduate School of Design. With grants from the National Institute of Mental Health and the Carnegie Corporation, he conducted research in creativity and developed training programs in problem solving. Mr. Straus also coauthored the bestseller *How to Make Meetings Work* (Jove Books, 1976).

David Straus lives in Cambridge, Massachusetts, with his wife, Patricia. They have two daughters, Sara Landis and Rebecca Straus.

## Berrett-Koehler Publishers

B ERRETT-KOEHLER is an independent publisher of books, periodicals, and other publications at the leading edge of new thinking and innovative practice on work, business, management, leadership, stewardship, career development, human resources, entrepreneurship, and global sustainability.

Since the company's founding in 1992, we have been committed to supporting the movement toward a more enlightened world of work by publishing books, periodicals, and other publications that help us to integrate our values with our work and work lives, and to create more humane and effective organizations.

We have chosen to focus on the areas of work, business, and organizations, because these are central elements in many people's lives today. Furthermore, the work world is going through tumultuous changes, from the decline of job security to the rise of new structures for organizing people and work. We believe that change is needed at all levels—individual, organizational, community, and global—and our publications address each of these levels.

We seek to create new lenses for understanding organizations, to legitimize topics that people care deeply about but that current business orthodoxy censors or considers secondary to bottom-line concerns, and to uncover new meaning, means, and ends for our work and work lives.

See next pages for other publications
from Berrett-Koehler Publishers

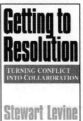

## PeopleSmart
### Developing Your Interpersonal Intelligence

Mel Silberman, Ph.D.,
with Freda Hansberg, Ph.D.

Everyone is in the people business because all of us deal with other people all the time. This eminently practical guide details eight essential skills of interpersonal intelligence and provides a powerful plan for becoming more effective in every relationship—with supervisors, coworkers, family, and friends.

Paperback original, 300 pages • ISBN 1-57675-091-4
Item #50914-415  $16.95

## Love 'Em or Lose 'Em
### Getting Good People to Stay, Second Edition

Beverly Kaye and Sharon Jordan-Evans

Regardless of economic swings or unemployment statistics,you need to keep your stars on your team. In this revised and updated edition of the bestselling classic, Kaye and Jordan-Evans explore the truth behind the dissatisfactions of many of today's workers and offer strategies that managers can use to address their concerns and keep them on the team.

Paperback original, 300 pages • ISBN 1-57675-140-6
Item # 51406-415  $18.95

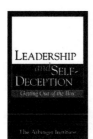

## Leadership and Self-Deception
### Getting Out of the Box

The Arbinger Institute

*Leadership and Self-Deception* reveals that there are only two ways for leaders to be: the source of leadership problems or the source of leadership success. The authors identify self-deception as the underlying cause of leadership failure and show how any leader can become a consistent catalyst of success.

Hardcover, 175 pages • 1-57675-094-9
Item #50949-415  $22.00

Paperback • 1-57675-174-0 • Item #51740-415  $14.95

**Berrett-Koehler Publishers**
PO Box 565, Williston, VT 05495-9900
Call toll-free! **800-929-2929** 7 am-9 pm Eastern Standard Time
Or fax your order to 802-864-7627
For fastest service order online: **www.bkconnection.com**

# Spread the word!

Berrett-Koehler books and audios are available at quantity discounts for orders of 10 or more copies.

## How to Make Collaboration Work

Powerful Ways to Build Consensus, Solve Problems, and Make Decisions

David Straus

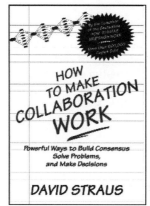

Paperback, 250 pages
ISBN 1-57675-128-7
Item #51287-415  $14.95

To find out about discounts on orders of 10 or more copies for individuals, corporations, institutions, and organizations, please call us toll-free at (800) 929-2929.

To find out about our discount programs for resellers, please contact our Special Sales department at (415) 288-0260; Fax: (415) 362-2512. Or email us at bkpub@bkpub.com.

**Berrett-Koehler Publishers**
PO Box 565, Williston, VT 05495-9900
Call toll-free! **800-929-2929** 7 am-9 pm Eastern Standard Time
Or fax your order to 802-864-7627
For fastest service order online: **www.bkconnection.com**